DICK

James Sharpe is Professor of History at York University and is a leading expert on the history of crime in pre-modern England. He was a founder member of the International Association for the History of Crime and Criminal Justice, and currently serves on its committee. He has also acted as director for an Economic and Social Research Council-funded project on the history of violence in England, 1600–1800. Previous publications include *Crime in seventeenth-century England: a County Study*, and *The Bewitching of Anne Gunter* (Profile). He is married with two children.

DICK TURPIN

The myth of the English highwayman

JAMES SHARPE

P

PROFILE BOOKS

This paperback edition published in 2005

First published in Great Britain in 2004 by
Profile Books Ltd
58A Hatton Garden
London ECIN 8LX
www.profilebooks.co.uk

3 5 7 9 10 8 6 4 2

Typeset in Poliphilus by MacGuru
info@macguru.org.uk

Printed and bound in Great Britain by
Bookmarque Ltd, Croydon, Surrey

A CIP catalogue record for this book is available
from the British Library.

ISBN 1 86197 418 3

For Freddie

As a warning against bad men

CONTENTS

PREFACE

Dick Turpin has been in my thoughts for a long time. My first researches as a historian of crime were carried out on seventeenth-century England, but from an early stage I broadened out, backwards into the late sixteenth century, and forwards into the early eighteenth. Both of these periods, as far as criminality is concerned, have their distinctive features. Those of the late sixteenth century need not detain us. Those of the early eighteenth include, firstly, insofar as we can reconstruct these things, changes in patterns of crime; secondly, and more certainly, changes in punishment, and hence, thirdly, changes in official perceptions of how crime might be combated. And, fourthly, changes, connected with an explosion in printed materials, in how crime and criminals were portrayed in the books, pamphlets, plays and newspapers of the period. From an early stage it struck me that the criminal career, trial, and execution of Dick Turpin drew a number of these themes together.

This feeling became deeper, and much better informed, when I had to focus my ideas on Turpin after agreeing in the late 1980s to give a lecture on him in one of York University's Open Course Lecture Series. This also introduced me to William Harrison Ainsworth, the man who, roughly a century after Turpin was executed, created the mythical Turpin who is currently a much more familiar figure than the historical one. Pursuing this theme further, and giving the occasional public talk on Turpin and the Turpin legend, not only convinced me of the interest of the theme, but also led me to ponder on how the disjuncture between the historical and the mythical Turpin, and the way in which England's best-known highwayman was constantly being recreated, reflected on the uses and meanings of history in modern Britain. Writing a book on Turpin seemed the only way to get history's most famous Essex Man off my mind.

While putting this book together I have benefited from the resources, and the helpfulness of the staff, of the British Library, the J. B. Morrell Library of the University of York, York Minster Library, the Gurney Library of the Borthwick Institute of Historical Research, York, the Public Record Office, London, York City Archives, the East Riding Archive Office, the Essex Record Office, and York Castle Museum. I have also benefited from correspondence with that great Turpin scholar, Derek Barlow. Once again, my wife, Krista Cowman, has been a source of support and advice.

I have decided to dispense with a formal structure of footnotes in this book, but any interested reader can follow the sources I have used by examining the notes and references at its end.

And, finally, a personal observation. Although I am not a native of that part of the country, I began my career as a historian working on the archives of the county of Essex. There is, as I write, every probability that I will end that career at York. There is a certain irony that, even if I have not exactly followed either Dick Turpin's footsteps or Black Bess's hoofprints, my professional life has followed a similar geographical trajectory to that of the man whose career and later reputation form the subject matter of this book.

Stillingfleet, North Yorkshire

chapter *one*

YORK, APRIL 1739

At least he died well, in what the eighteenth century considered the appropriate manner for its condemned criminals. Determined to look his best when he met his end, he had, a few days previously, bought himself a new frock coat and a pair of pumps. He had also, as a further preparation, on the day before his execution appointed five men as his mourners, and given them three pounds and ten shillings to be shared among them for following the cart that would carry him to the gallows and for overseeing his subsequent interment. He distributed hatbands and gloves to several other people, and left a gold ring and two pairs of shoes and clogs to a married woman with whom he had consorted, despite reports that he had a wife and child living in the south, while he lived under an assumed identity at the Humberside township of Brough.

On Saturday 7 April, the day of execution, he was carried in a cart, his mourners behind him, from the county gaol at York Castle through the centre of the city, up Micklegate, through Micklegate Bar, and on to what a contemporary source describes as 'a fair broad street, well paved on both sides'; in fact, the first few hundred yards of the road to Tadcaster. He was accompanied in the cart by the other man sentenced to death a fortnight previously at the Yorkshire assizes, John Stead, like him convicted for horse-stealing. Of John Stead we know little. But Stead's companion in the cart, up to a few weeks before known to his captors as John Palmer, was a rather more significant figure: the notorious highwayman Richard Turpin, a year or two previously England's most wanted criminal, with a £200 reward for murder on his head. Sir George Cooke, sheriff of Yorkshire and the official responsible for the smooth running of the execution, was later to claim twenty pounds in expenses for conveying Turpin and Stead 'under a strong guard' to the place of execution, evidence of concern over an attempted escape or rescue. In the event, such worries proved misplaced. Turpin, so the description of his execution tells us, acted out the role fate had allotted to him, 'behav'd himself with amazing assurance', and 'bow'd to the spectators as he passed'. His and Stead's last morning was probably a cold one: certainly Arthur Jessop, an apothecary living at Wooldale over in the West Riding, had noted in his diary that the previous day had seen 'a blustering cold wind, rain hail and snow'. But, despite the circumstances, Turpin was evidently determined to die game.

The place of execution, known in imitation of its better-known metropolitan equivalent as Tyburn, was at the Knavesmire, about a mile outside the city and on the left-hand side of the road heading west. The Knavesmire will be most familiar to the modern reader as the site of York racecourse, and, indeed, it had by 1739 already acquired this function. But criminals had long been executed there, and a small stone currently marks the spot where the gallows stood. These gallows, like those at the more famous Tyburn in London, took the form of a triangle laid on its side, and held above the ground at each corner by a vertical beam, a design which led to the York gallows being nicknamed 'The Three-Legged Mare'. A ladder was placed against one of the horizontal beams of the wooden triangle, upon which Turpin was expected to stand. He mounted the ladder, and managed to control a trembling in his left leg, 'which he stamped down with an air', after which he looked round about him with 'undaunted courage'.

Turpin then turned to speak to the executioner, and it is here that we confront the first of the several ironies we shall encounter in the story of Dick Turpin. York did not have a permanent hangman. It was the custom at each York assize to pardon one of the prisoners who had been sentenced to death on condition that he acted as executioner for the other capitally convicted prisoners. On this occasion the former prisoner acting as hangman was a Thomas Hadfield, who had been pardoned after being sentenced to death for highway robbery: thus the most famous highwayman in English history ended his life by being hanged by one of his own kind. After a few words (we may dismiss accounts that claimed the two men talked for half an hour) Turpin 'threw himself off the ladder, and expired directly'. As the pamphlet account of his execution published shortly after his death put it, Turpin 'went off this stage with as much intrepidity and unconcern, as if he had been taking horse to go on a journey'.

The York where Turpin spent the last few weeks of his life was very much a city 'on the up'. In a striking prefiguration of what was to happen to a number of British urban centres in the late twentieth century, York, having experienced the doldrums of de-industrialization and economic stagnation after its status as a cloth-manufacturing centre collapsed in the sixteenth century, reinvented itself in the late seventeenth as a centre of services for the local elite. Francis Drake, from 1727 city surgeon at York and author of a massive history of the city first published three years before Turpin's execution, gave a number of reasons for this development. York was much cheaper to live in than London, it offered good educational facilities for the children of the gentry and the better-off townsfolk, and it offered a wide range of leisure activities to people of taste and fashion, among them a company of stage players and, of course, the races. York's new status as a place of resort for the fashionable was symbolised by the Assembly Rooms, the creation of the aristocrat-cum-architect Richard Boyle, third Earl of Burlington, lying at the top of Blake Street in the heart of the city, and opened in time for race week 1732. In the same year the city council, who had already in 1719 improved and beautified Lord Mayor's Walk, skirting York's northern city wall, opened New Walk, along the banks of the Ouse between Fishergate and Fulford, to provide yet another location where persons of taste and quality might promenade.

The early eighteenth century witnessed a further, if considerably less genteel, demonstration of York's growing regional importance and civic pride. This was the construction of a new county gaol, built in 1701 and paid for by a county tax raised by private Act of Parliament. Previously, as was the case in most English counties in the period, the county gaol for Yorkshire had been located in an old castle. But its structure had deteriorated badly and it had been decided to replace it with a new purpose-built prison, according to Drake a 'most magnificent structure … a building so noble and compleat as exceeds all others, of its kind, in Britain; perhaps in Europe'. Drake claimed that 'the justices of the peace for this county have of late years taken great care that this gaol should be as neat and convenient within, as it is noble without; by allowing of straw for the felons, and raising their beds which before used to be upon the ground'. The authorities' solicitude for the prisoners extended to the construction of a chapel, and to the provision of an infirmary and a salaried surgeon. One doubts if Turpin was much impressed by any of this, or that his architectural sensibilities were sufficiently developed for his being able to take pleasure from spending his last few weeks in what was the only baroque prison ever to be built in England. But at least while he awaited trial and, subsequently, execution, he was held in what was, by the standards of the time, a well-run and advanced penal institution.

The final stages of Turpin's time in York Castle were evidently very sociable. An anonymous 'Letter from York', published in the *General Evening Post* of 8 March 1739 (the letter was dated six days earlier) reported of Turpin that

> a great concourse of people flock to see him, and they all give him money. He seems very sure that nobody is alive that can hurt him, and told the gentleman with whom he used to hunt, that he hoped to have another day's sport with him yet. And that if he had thought they would have made such a rout with him he would have owned it before ... He is put every night into the condemned hold, which is a very strong place ...

'Since he was suspected to be Turpin', ran another 'Letter from York', in this instance dated 23 March, 'the whole countrey have flock'd here to see him, and have been very liberal to him, insomuch as he has had wine constantly before him.' The same source noted that the gaoler at York Castle 'has made £100 by selling liquors to him and his visitors'.

Further confirmation that the condemned Turpin was a centre of public attention comes from one of the descriptions of his execution. This, commenting on how the prospect of death seemed so often to hold few terrors for men who 'for many years successively, have employ'd all their talents and endeavours in robbing, plundering, and destroying the lives and properties of their fellow creatures', and remarked that this was also true of 'the unhappy Turpin', who

> being committed prisoner to York Castle, as has been before related, lived in as much pleasure as the liberties of the prison would afford, eating, drinking and carousing with anybody that would spend their time with him. Neither did he alter his behaviour even after his condemnation. After it was rumour'd abroad, that he was the Turpin who had render'd himself so notorious for his robberies in the southern parts of England, abundance of people from all parts resorted daily to see him … he continu'd his mirthful humour to the last, spending his time in joking, drinking and telling stories.

It was always felt necessary to prepare the condemned spiritually for their end, and accordingly a clergyman (we do not know his identity) offered Turpin 'serious remonstrances and admonitions', but to no avail. Turpin ignored his efforts, 'and whatever remorse he had on his conscience for his past villanies, he kept it to himself, not expressing the least concern at the melancholy circumstances he was in'.

Those circumstances became definitively melancholy on the morning of Saturday 7 April 1739. The humour, the joking, drinking and story-telling came to an end. His corpse was left hanging on the gallows until three in the afternoon to ensure that he was really dead, when it was cut down, and laid out in the Blue Boar tavern in Castlegate. Eighteenth-century England had hanged another criminal.

Another criminal, perhaps, but not *any* other criminal. Dick Turpin is one of that select band of figures from England's past (others might include Henry VIII, Queen Victoria, Sir Winston Churchill and, interestingly, Robin Hood) who are instantly recognisable to everyone. Even the most subliterate fourteen-year-old will have heard of Turpin, and will be able to recognise the image of the man in the tricorn hat with his frock coat, pistols and riding boots, and will be able to inform the questioner that Turpin had a horse called Black Bess, on whom he rode from London to York. More generally, the public at large imagine Turpin as a courageous and romantic figure, a man of considerable daring, a defier of corrupt officialdom and a man who, like Robin Hood, robbed the rich to help the poor. But it is in legend, in a mythologised view of history, that Dick Turpin flourishes: if his image is instantly recognisable to everyone, few people could give any very precise details about him.

This is a pity, as Turpin's story, which can be reconstructed from newspaper reports of his period, from two pamphlets published immediately after his death, and from a scattering of archival records, is an instructive one. This process of recon-struction may not tell us much about Turpin's personality, but it does give us the opportunity to put together a remarkable crimi-nal biography, a tale of violent robberies from houses, of high-way robberies, of murder, and, eventually, of the horse-thefts that led to his execution. But with Turpin we are not just wit-nessing the career of one criminal: we also gain an entry into the workings of both the criminal-justice system and the criminality of the early eighteenth century, of the law-and-order machine on the one hand and the world of organised crime on the other. The former, with its lack of a professional police force and its dependence on public execution as the main bulwark against serious offenders, has been much misunderstood; the latter, much romanticised. So writing a book about Turpin involves not just telling the story of a well-documented criminal, but also involves understanding the very distinctive forms of crime and punishment of Turpin's England, when both organised crime in something like the modern sense and the identification of crime as a political issue, a theme so familiar in the modern world, were emerging for the first time. And it was also a period in which there was an avid taste for tales about criminals.

But, if Dick Turpin's story opens up some major areas of history, it also throws light on that other way of constructing and remembering the past: legend. Turpin is a figure who is instantly recognisable to the bulk of the population, and around whom a potent mythology has gathered. None of this would have been apparent to those who apprehended, guarded, exe-cuted, or gave evidence against him in 1739. Yes, he was a noto-rious criminal: but one or two of those emerged every year in the eighteenth century, to enjoy a brief fame before they, too, ended their career on the gallows. Yes, a couple of pamphlets were written after Turpin's execution, but this was pretty standard, and numerous such ephemeral publications recounting the careers and recording the last hours of dozens of now long-forgotten criminals survive in the nation's research libraries. But it is Turpin we remember, Turpin who has passed into the popular consciousness, not the dozens of others. So with Dick Turpin we encounter two other issues. The first is the nature of legend, of how it gets created and perpetuated, an issue that also leads us into contemplating the nature of fame. The second is the relationship between history and legend, and, by extension, of how the two operate in our modern culture, and how we draw on both of them to imagine our past. For what if Turpin were not the swashbuckling figure of legend, but rather an unpleasant and violent criminal as unheroic as any who commit crimes today? What if he were not the dashing silk-clad dandy of legend, but rather a heavily pockmarked man of average height? And what, indeed, if the ride to York and Black Bess were nothing but fictions? Why, then, should a totally fictitious version of the past prove so pervasive?

So in thinking about Dick Turpin, we will involve ourselves in a lot more than a catalogue of highway robberies. In the centuries following his death, the man whose body swung from the gallows by York racecourse on that chill April morning was to have much more than that to answer for.

But the legend lay in an unimagined future when Turpin was

hanged. Indeed, until six weeks before his execution, nobody had suspected that the alleged horse-thief being held in York Castle was Richard Turpin. He was known as John Palmer and, if the revelation of Turpin's true identity was a stroke of monstrous bad luck, the only reason he was drawn into the criminal-justice system in the first place was because of an act of childish petulance on his part, an act that might be read as revealing an irrational temper and a taste for violence.

John Palmer had arrived in Yorkshire in or about June 1737. William Harris, keeper of the Ferry Inn at Brough, just north of the River Humber, deposed to three justices of the peace for the East Riding how at roughly that time

> one John Palmer came to this informant's house in Brough aforesaid and boarded with this informant at Brough aforesaid four or five months and during that time went from this exami-nant's house over the water [i.e. across the River Humber] into the county of Lincoln at divers times and the said times returned to this informant's house att Brough aforesaid with sev-erall horses at a time which he sold and disposed of to divers persons in the county of York. And this informant inquireing of the said John Palmer the place of his abode the said John Palmer told this informant that he lived at Long Sutton with his father and that his sister kept his father's house there and the rea-son for leaving his father was for debt and was feared of being arrested by bailiffs and said that if they once catched him they would kill him.

Harris replied that 'it would be very hard to kill a man for debt and that he went unarmed', but Palmer, his tongue possibly loosened by beer, told Harris that 'if he went over the water with him the said Palmer, he w'ld shew him such a pair of pistolls as he this informant never saw in his life and that he did not fear the bailiffs ... before they'd catch me a great deal of blood shall be spent'.

The reason why Harris was giving evidence about the man he knew as John Palmer was that the previous day, 2 October 1738, Palmer had threatened to shoot a labourer named John Robinson. Robinson, a Brough man, gave his evidence with another Brough resident, Abraham Green. The justices noted that

> this informant Abraham Green saith that John Palmer of Wel-
> ton aforesaid did on the second day of October instant at
> Brough above said with a gunn kill a tame fowl which did
> belong to Francis Hall of Brough aforesaid neatherd [i.e.
> cowherd] and did throw the fowl into the fields of Elloughton
> in the said Riding and Brough aforesaid and this informant
> John Robinson saith that he did see John Palmer on the said sec-
> ond day of October att Brough aforesaid kill the said fowl
> belonging to the said Francis Hall and he reprimanding the said
> John Palmer concerning the same, he the said John Palmer did
> threaten to shoot this informant.

Robert Appleton, Clerk of the Peace for the East Riding and a man who was subsequently to take an important part in secur-ing Turpin's conviction, later provided details about this inci-dent. Palmer, who by now was clearly well integrated in the society of the area, 'often went out a hunting and shooting with several gentlemen in the neighbourhood'. On this occasion, he

was returning from shooting, and, perhaps having had a disap-
pointing day's sport, shot one of another man's cocks in the
street. Reprimanded for so doing, Turpin replied to the man
criticising his conduct that 'if he would only stay whilst he had
charged his piece, he would shoot him too'.

Hall and Robinson presumably complained to the East
Riding justices, three of whom (George Crowle, Hugh Bethell
and Marmaduke Constable) came to Brough to take written
depositions about the incident and to bind Palmer over to keep
the peace. Matters should have ended there: Palmer's shooting of
the cock and threatening of Robinson, in the light of Hall and
Robinson's complaint, obviously merited some official sanction.
Conversely, binding over to keep the peace was a fairly common
occurrence, and Palmer's conduct had not caused damage to
human life or limb. But being bound over to keep the peace
meant finding sureties, and Palmer refused to do so. So, the three
justices took the most obvious course open to them and had
Palmer committed to the House of Correction at Beverley
where petty-nuisance offenders were regularly held. Palmer,
escorted by the parish constable of Welton, rode there on his
own horse, which was stabled at the Blue Bell inn on arrival at
Beverley. It remains unclear why Palmer was unwilling to find
sureties, or why, given that he was in fact the hardened criminal
Richard Turpin, he made no attempt to escape. Perhaps he was
suffering from a lack of confidence, or, conversely, possibly was
convinced that the matter was too insignificant to be worth
worrying about.

Our account of what happened next is very dependent on
Robert Appleton's version of events. According to Appleton,
the three justices became interested in what they were begin-

ning to hear about Palmer's reputation in the locality. The innkeeper William Harris had commented on how Palmer had crossed the Humber into Lincolnshire on numerous occasions, and had returned 'with several horses which he sold and disposed of to divers persons in the county of York', while a number of other people in the area had noted the peculiar pattern of Palmer's movements. There was also some uncertainty about how exactly Palmer made his living. Richard Grassby, later giving evidence at Turpin's trial, declared that the man he had known as John Palmer 'had no settled way of living, that I know of at all, though a dealer, yet he was a stranger, and lived like a gentleman', and being pressed again to describe 'in what manner of way used he to support himself or, how did he live', replied simply, 'he lived like a gentleman'. Overall, Appleton tells us, there was enough opacity about Palmer's doings to make the trio of justices suspicious that he might have been involved in crime.

> The gentlemen having taken several informations from persons of Brough and Welton, about Palmer's frequently going into Lincolnshire, and usually returning with plenty of money, and several horses, which he sold or exchanged in Yorkshire, had just reason to suspect, that he was either a highwayman or a horse-stealer; and ... the next day went to the said John Palmer, and examined him again, touching where he lived, and to what business he was brought up.

Palmer replied that he was a butcher by trade, and that up to about two years previously he had lived at Long Sutton in Lincolnshire, at his father's house, and that he had fallen heavily into debt 'for sheep that proved rotten', and that he had accord-ingly absconded and come to live in Yorkshire.

The three justices proved to be unusually assiduous in pur-suing the matter. They directed Appleton to 'send a messenger into Lincolnshire, to enquire into the truth of this matter', which he did, sending a letter to a Lincolnshire justice of the peace, a Mr Delamere, who lived at Long Sutton. If falling foul of the authorities by shooting Francis Hall's cock and threaten-ing John Robinson was Turpin's first mistake, admitting resi-dence in Long Sutton was his second. Delamere replied that a John Palmer had indeed resided at Long Sutton, although his father had never been a resident of the parish. This Palmer, wrote Delamere, had been suspected for sheep-theft and had escaped the local constable's custody while being investigated for that offence, while the Lincolnshire justice had also taken several depositions against Palmer for suspected horse-theft. Appleton passed this information on to George Crowle, who by now thought Palmer too serious an offender to be kept in Beverley House of Correction. Crowle required Palmer to find sureties to appear at the next assizes at York, and when Palmer refused to do so had him committed to York Castle, whence he was sent in handcuffs and under guard on 16 October.

We know of three horse thefts that Turpin, or John Palmer as he was still known in Yorkshire and Lincolnshire, commit-ted there. The first of these, although the least germane to our story, is the most bizarre. The horse in question, described as a 'bay brown gelding', belonged to Charles Townsend, son of Thomas Townsend in Pinchbeck in Lincolnshire. Pinchbeck is about twelve miles from Long Sutton, and the younger Townsend was, like his father, in holy orders, and probably acting as the older man's curate. Turpin stole his horse in July 1737, but instead of taking it across the Humber to sell in Yorkshire, he took it with him on a surprise visit to his family, his father, John Turpin, then being landlord of the Blue Bell inn at Hempstead in Essex. When Turpin returned to the north, for whatever reason he left the horse he had stolen from Charles Townsend behind him. Everyone in Hempstead was fully aware of the identity of Turpin senior's son, and the sudden arrival of a strange horse in his stable was calculated to arouse suspicion. Interested parties in Essex conducted enquiries about the horse, which was found to belong to Charles Townsend, and John Turpin accordingly found himself on 12 September 1738 committed to gaol in Essex to await trial for horse-theft. He betrayed a gaol break planned by a group of his fellow-prisoners in early February 1739, a circumstance which probably aided the charges against him being thrown out at Chelmsford assizes on 5 March.

Turpin's return to Lincolnshire after his visit home seems to have been the point at which he dabbled in sheep-theft, although the only evidence we have of these activities is Justice Delamere's letter, as reported by Richard Appleton. This suggests that Turpin was actually arrested for the offence, but escaped. But he did so without a horse, which was obviously going to impede his progress to Yorkshire. His solution was to steal three horses at Heckington, about twenty miles from Long Sutton on the road north. The horses, a mare, her foal and a gelding, belonged to Thomas Creasy, who discovered on 17 or 18 August that the three horses, which he had last seen on Heckington common a day previously, were missing. Creasy hired men to ride in a forty-mile radius around Heckington to make enquiries if the horses had been seen, and also, employing a technique that was being increasingly resorted to by those who had had goods stolen from them, advertised the lost horses in the market towns of the area. These measures proved fruitless, but, as Creasy was later to explain at Turpin's trial, he had a lucky break.

> One John Baxter, a neighbour of mine told me, that he had been at Pocklington fair in Yorkshire and laying all night at Brough, he happened to hear of a man that was taken up and sent to the House of Correction at Beverley for shooting a game cock, who had such a mare and foal as mine. Upon which information I came to Ferraby [i.e. Ferriby] near Beverley and put up my horse at Richard Grassby's who kept a publick house; and began to enquire of him about ye mare and foal. Who told me there was such like a mare and foal in their neighbourhood which I thought by the description he gave me, to be mine; so then I told him, I was come to enquire about such a mare and foal.

Grassby showed Creasy the two horses, which he promptly claimed as his own. Richard Grassby also told Creasy that Palmer had ridden on a black gelding with a star on its forehead, similar to the one he had lost, when he had been committed to Beverley House of Correction. He then went to Beverley, discovered that the gelding was still being stabled at the Blue Bell, and again claimed it as his own. Creasy obtained a justice's order to recover his horse, and subsequently showed it to Carey Gill, the constable of Welton.

Although the mare and the foal were still at Welton, Turpin

had already been able to sell them on. The buyer was Captain George Dawson of Brigadier General Harrison's Regiment. This unit was stationed at Bristol, but Dawson was on leave at Ferriby, some two miles from Welton, when he saw a man walking a mare and a foal. According to the account he gave the court at Turpin's trial, he saw the two horses when a man was walking them, who, on enquiry, said that they 'belonged to one Palmer'. Turpin, in his identity of Palmer, 'was coming up the street … who told me it was his mare and foal, and that they were bred in Lincolnshire'. Dawson asked if Palmer was willing to sell the foal, to which Palmer replied that he would prefer to sell the mare and the foal together. Dawson said he 'had no occasion for the mare, only for the foal', and when Palmer responded that he wanted three guineas for the foal, Dawson replied that this was too much, and offered two. The negotiations broke off, but were resumed when the two men came across each other again a little later. Turpin obviously had a good sales technique ('the prisoner being a little pressing about it', in Dawson's words), for Dawson decided to take the mare with the foal for four guineas, also throwing in 'a horse of no great value'. 'Being obliged to go to my regiment', Dawson explained, 'I left the place soon after', leaving the mare and the foal in the custody of Richard Grassby. Dawson's statement was later to prove crucial at Turpin's trial.

By the autumn of 1738 evidence was therefore building up against John Palmer, prisoner in York Castle, with rumours of his shady goings-on now becoming crystallised by the specific accusation that he had stolen three horses from Thomas Creasy. Horse-theft was a capital offence, but it was unusual for a first offender to be executed for it. John Palmer, despite his lack of

THE
TRIAL

Of the Notorious Highwayman
Richard Turpin,

At *York* Affizes, on the 22d Day of *March*, 1739, before the Hon. Sir WILLIAM CHAPPLE, Kt. Judge of Affize, and one of His Majefty's Juftices of the Court of King's Bench.

Taken down in Court by Mr. THOMAS KYLL, Profeffor of Short Hand.

To which is prefix'd,
An exact Account of the faid *Turpin*, from his firft coming into *Yorkfhire*, to the Time of his being committed Prifoner to *York* Caftle; communicated by Mr. APPLETON of *Beverley*, Clerk of the Peace for the *Eaft-Riding* of the faid County.

With a Copy of a Letter which *Turpin* received from his Father, while under Sentence of Death.

To which is added,
His Behaviour at the Place of Execution, on *Saturday* the 7th of *April*, 1739. Together with the whole Confeffion he made to the Hangman at the Gallows; wherein he acknowledg'd himfelf guilty of the Facts for which he fuffer'd, own'd the Murder of Mr. *Thompfon*'s Servant on *Epping*-Foreft, and gave a particular Account of feveral Robberies which he had committed.

Y O R K :
Printed by W A R D and C H A N D L E R; and Sold at their Shop without *Temple-Bar*, *London*; and in *Coney-Street*, *York*, 1739. (Price Six-pence.)

1. The title page of a pamphlet published at York immediately after Turpin's trial and execution. This is the main source for the last few months of his life (© Dean and Chapter of York: By kind permission).

contacts in Yorkshire and Lincolnshire, and despite such evidence as Justice Delamere from Long Sutton might have been
able to provide, might well have been able to escape the noose in
that lottery which the workings of the eighteenthcentury criminaljustice system constituted. Richard Turpin, the notorious
malefactor, would have stood little chance of escaping execution
on this or any other indictment for felony.

Early in February 1739 Turpin wrote a letter to his brotherinlaw, identified as 'Pompr' Rivernall, who like Turpin's father
lived at Hempstead in Essex. Rivernall's Christian name is
uncertain (his surname also appears in variant spellings),
although it is known that he was married to Turpin's sister
Dorothy. The letter was addressed to the Blue Bell inn at Hempstead, and it is probable that John Turpin's daughter and her
husband were running the establishment while its owner, John
Turpin, languished in Chelmsford gaol. The letter (despite
claims to the contrary) has not survived, but it seems likely that
it was meant to let the family know that Turpin was held in
York Castle, and to ask them to mobilise character witnesses on
behalf of the fictitious John Palmer from the London area.

In this period the postal service in the modern sense did not
exist. Letters were sent to local post offices (normally located in
inns or shops) where they were kept until their recipients came
to collect them, the recipient being responsible for paying the
postal charges. Rivernall was alerted to the letter's arrival, but
saw the York post stamp on the letter, and refused to take it,

declaring that 'he had no correspondent at York'. It may be simply that he wished to avoid the relevant postal charges, although there is also a possibility that he recognised the handwriting, and was anxious to avoid any enmeshment in the affairs of his decidedly problematic brother-in-law. Whatever Rivernall's motives, there was somebody who definitely did recognise the handwriting, another Hempstead resident named James Smith. As Smith explained at Turpin's trial,

> happening to be at the post office where I saw a letter directed to Turpin's brother-in-law who, as I was informed, would not loose [i.e. loosen, take] the letter and pay postage, upon that account taking particular notice thereof, I thought at first I remembered the superscription, and concluded it to be the handwriting of the prisoner, Turpin; whereupon I carried the letter before a Magistrate who broke the same open (the letter was subscribed John Palmer) I found it sent from York Castle; I had seen several of Dick Turpin's bills and knew his hand.

Smith, in fact, had taught Turpin, at that point his younger schoolmate, to write while he was at school. His presence in Hempstead post office was a piece of massive bad luck for the highwayman.

An earlier statement by James Smith, taken at York on 23 February, presumably the day of his arrival in the city, told how the letter had been sent to the post office at Saffron Walden, the main market town in the area, after Rivernall had refused to take it, and the justice of the peace whom Smith had alerted, Thomas Stubbing of Helion's Bumpstead, had paid the postage on it. After he and Smith had examined the letter, and

Smith had expressed his opinion that it was written in Turpin's hand, Stubbing and three other justices asked Smith 'to go to York Castle to see whether it was the said Turpin or not'. Smith subsequently swore to the York authorities that the person shown to him as John Palmer 'is Richard Turpin and no other person'. He declared that he had been raised in the same township as Turpin, had been to school with him, 'and hath constantly for several years since been in company with him till these three or four years'. In fact, Smith's later testimony at Turpin's trial suggests that he identified him in some sort of forerunner of a modern identity parade: asked if he had recognised Turpin on his coming to York Castle, Smith replied, 'Yes I did, upon the first view of him, and pointed him out from amongst the rest of the other prisoners.'

Smith's identification on 23 February 1739 of John Palmer as Richard Turpin suddenly moved the whole affair from a local to a national level. John Palmer the horsethief was a matter of concern to the county authorities of the East Riding of Yorkshire and of Lincolnshire. The discovery that Palmer was, in fact, Richard Turpin, once England's most notorious criminal, and a man who still had £200 on his head, was clearly a matter of concern to central government. Thomas Place, Recorder [i.e. chief legal official] of York, and one of the three men who had taken James Smith's evidence, certainly thought so. The day after Smith arrived in York from Essex, Place wrote to the Duke of Newcastle, Secretary of State for the Southern Department:

My Lord,
On the 16th of October last a fellow was committed to York Castle on suspicion of stealing sheep and horses by the name of

John Palmer. From the information taken yesterday before me and the other two gentlemen whose names are subscribed to it (of which the enclosed is a true copy) and from many other circumstances concurring it appeared that the person is Turpin against whom a proclamation issued: he long persisted in denying his knowledge of the informer and of every thing contained in the information. I went to him again in the evening he then confessed to me that the information was true and that he was Turpin and that he had been in the neighbourhood of Hull for about the last two years so that I think no doubt can remain as to the identity of the person. I thought it my duty to give your Grace the most early notice of this. Orders are to be given for his strict confinement till his Majesty's pleasure concerning him can be known.

Thomas Place was evidently aware of the importance of the man held in York Castle, and was clearly anxious that central government should know that Turpin was now in custody

The 1730s were possibly the earliest point in English history when the central government, and certainly somebody as august as Thomas Pelham-Holles, Duke of Newcastle, one of the most powerful politicians in England and a future prime minister, would take direct interest in the fate of a highway robber. It was at about this time that something akin to the modern concept of law and order as a political issue was starting to take root, and the apparently unchecked activities of criminals like Turpin might be used as ammunition by a political opposition anxious to discredit the government. And in 1739 the government, presided over by Sir Robert Walpole, was in no mind to offer the opposition any such opportunities. Walpole, widely regarded by later historians as the first approximation to a prime minister in the modern sense, had early in his ascendancy, and that of his party, the Whigs, enjoyed almost untrammelled power founded on large parliamentary majorities. Opposition had, however, become strident, focussed, and nearly successful in the excise crisis of 1733, which was followed by a hotly contested general election in 1734. After that date, the Walpole administration was permanently on the defensive. In April 1739 the main concern was with foreign affairs: Walpole was a great believer in keeping Britain out of warfare, but from 1737 popular pressure had been building up for a war against Spain. This pressure eventually resulted in that most mismanaged of conflicts which is remembered quaintly in the textbooks as the War of Jenkins' Ear. But domestic issues were permanently of importance, and Walpole's administration was sensitive to any challenge, even one so apparently insignificant as the continued freedom of a solitary highwayman.

This was a time of growing anxiety about crime that, by about 1750, was to lead to England's first law-and-order debate. So in 1739 any political administration claiming to operate on a sound basis would be expected to protect honest citizens from criminals, and it was evident that many honest citizens, or at least many pundits, were convinced that Walpole's government was failing in this fundamental task. Thus the 30 July 1737 issue of *Common Sense*, a leading political periodical, had carried a piece which criticised the government for permitting 'the flagrant, undisturbed success of the infamous Turpin, who hath robbed in a manner, scarce ever known to before'. The journal deplored the want of public spirit that would allow a situation where 'a fellow, who is known to be a thief by the whole kingdom, shall for a long time rob us, and not only so, but to make jest of us, shall defy the laws and laugh at justice', an editorial comment making the suggestion of 'applying our idle soldiery for the security of the roads, as is done by the wise government in China'. These comments were made just over a month after the government, in a document appearing in the Duke of Newcastle's name, offered pardon to any of Turpin's accomplices who turned him in, and a reward of £200 'to any person or persons who shall discover the said criminal, so as he may be apprehended and convicted'. Catching and convicting Turpin was something that central government, and in particular the Duke of Newcastle, regarded as very much to be desired.

The reward for the apprehension of Turpin was offered in the wake of his having murdered Thomas Morris, servant to Henry Thompson, one of the Keepers of Epping Forest in Essex, while most of the highway robberies and other offences Turpin was wanted for when the reward was offered had been committed in the London area. Newcastle therefore envisaged bringing Turpin south for trial, and ordered Andrew Stone, the Under Secretary of State for the Southern Department and the duke's trusted servant, to get the opinion of Sir Dudley Ryder, the Attorney General, on the best course of action. Ryder wrote on 28 February that he had consulted such documentation as had been sent to him, and advised that even though he had not seen informations relating to the killing of Thomas Morris, the best course would be that 'it may be proper to give directions for his removal hither be Habeas Corpus, from York gaol, in order to be tried here'. It is a measure of the importance attached to convicting Turpin that central government was obviously acting very quickly and decisively, so that it appeared likely that Turpin would be tried in London or Essex for murder and highway robbery, rather than in York for horse-theft.

That Turpin was tried and executed in York was largely the work of George Crowle, one of those East Riding justices of the peace who had been called in when Palmer had shot Francis Hall's cock and threatened John Robinson at Brough in October 1738. Crowle was Member of Parliament for Hull, and as Parliament resumed its session on 1 February 1739 it is likely that he was in London from or before that date. He was a strong supporter of the Walpole administration, and had been given a place in the victualling office in recognition of his loyalty in 1733. He was thus well placed to influence the central authorities about the location of Turpin's trial. Some intriguing evidence exists in a submission made by the Treasury solicitor after Turpin's execution when the central authorities were having to consider the various claims made for a share of the reward money offered for Turpin's arrest and conviction. Crowle, according to this document,

> observes further that upon the first discovery of Turpin's being in York gaol, it was the Attorney General's opinion that he should be brought up here [i.e to London] to be tried which would have been a great expense to the Crown, and then doubtful whether he would have been convicted here, but upon the assurances that Mr Crowle gave the Attorney General that there was sufficient proof against him at York he gave his opinion and consented to his trial there, by which means a very large sum of money was saved to the Crown.

It is doubtful if cutting the costs of central government expendi-
ture was Crowle's major concern. Maybe some sort of local
pride, a feeling that Turpin had been apprehended by Yorkshire
justices and hence ought to be tried in Yorkshire, may have motivated him. More pertinent, perhaps, was the fact that Crowle
felt confident that if the trial were held in York, he would be able
to ensure that one of the members for the prosecution, a significant position given Turpin's importance, should be his younger
brother Richard, then an Attorney in the Inner Temple in London. Crowle could not have swung this minor act of nepotism
if the trial had taken place in Essex or London, and Richard
was not well established enough to ensure a place on a southern
prosecution team on the strength of his own reputation. Newcastle evidently fretted over the matter, and on 21 March sent a
messenger up to York with a copy of the Essex coroner's inquest
on Morris's death, and details of various robberies committed
by Turpin in the south, with a view, as the *York Courant* of 27
March 1739 put it, 'of removing him to Chelmsford, if he had
not been capitally convicted here'. But by that date Newcastle's
caution had been rendered otiose.

The York winter assizes opened on 19 March 1739,
although the time needed to deal with civil actions at the court
meant that Turpin's trial did not take place until Thursday 22
March. Turpin was indicted on two counts: firstly, for stealing
a mare worth three pounds and a foal worth twenty shillings,
and secondly for stealing a gelding worth three pounds, all
three animals being the property of Thomas Creasy. The
indictments both stated that the alleged offences had taken
place at Welton on 1 March 1739, and described the accused as
'John Palmer alias Pawmer alias Richard Turpin ... late of the

castle of York in the County of York labourer'. The wording
of the indictments is clearly absurd: the offences took place at
Heckington in Lincolnshire, not Welton in Yorkshire, and they
occurred in August 1738, not March 1739, at which point
Turpin had been incarcerated in York Castle for nearly five
months. And 'labourer' was a catch-all occupational label
applied to most of the male accused of the period.

The indictments against Turpin constitute a late example of
one of the great, and as yet not fully explained, peculiarities of
English criminal-court records of the early modern period. In
theory, the details of the crime committed as given on indictments should have been totally accurate: fifteenth-century legislation had established this principle, and this legislation was
backed by legal opinion, which declared that inaccuracies in the
wording of indictments could make a criminal charge void. Yet
a surprising number of indictments contained manifest factual
errors that did not, in practice, stand in the way of criminals
being convicted on capital charges. By the early eighteenth century, rising levels of bureaucratic efficiency and lower levels of
business meant that the details given on indictments were
becoming more accurate than they had been in earlier periods. It
is therefore surprising that Turpin was tried on what were technically invalid charges, and doubly surprising that such sloppy
drafting should have occurred when the accused was as important a criminal as Turpin, whose successful conviction was a
matter of some concern to the authorities.

The indictments were screened by the Grand Jury, a body of
gentry drawn from various parts of Yorkshire, whose responsi-
bility it was to determine that those indictments described criminal charges which were worth prosecuting. With Turpin's

indictments the Grand Jury decided that this was the case, marked them 'True Bill' on the back, and also listed there the names of the witnesses who were to be called against him: Thomas Creasy, Carey Gill, George Dawson, Esq., George Goodyear, James Smith, Edward Saward and Richard Grassby. Captain George Dawson, the soldier who had bought Thomas Creasy's foal and mare from Turpin, had, under central government direction, been given leave from his regiment to attend the assizes.

So on Thursday 22 March 1739 Richard Turpin, the notorious highwayman, stood trial in York on two counts of horse-theft. The outcome of the first item of the court's business could not have lifted his spirits: John Stead, also accused of horse-theft, aged thirty-eight and a native of Pontefract, was convicted, and by the same trial jury of twelve men that was to try Turpin. The assizes were fairly busy: the *London Evening Post* of 22–24 March said that there were twenty-three persons, including a John Palmer 'who has pass'd for Turpin, and made money by it' awaiting trial, and surviving recognizances, calling witnesses to give evidence against those standing trial, would support this kind of figure. According to the *York Courant* of 10 April, as well as Turpin and Stead being capitally convicted, a housebreaker named Naomi Hollings was reprieved after successfully claiming she was pregnant, Thomas Hadfield the highwayman was reprieved on condition that he acted as hangman, another man, Laurence Roberts, was also reprieved, and two others, John Munckman and John Robinson, were transported to the American colonies. Presiding over their trials and Turpin's was Sir William Chapple, an experienced, senior and respected judge in his early sixties.

Among those in the court was a York resident, Thomas Kyll, a self-styled 'Professor of Shorthand'. Kyll used his skills to good effect that Thursday, and took down full notes of the proceedings against Turpin, which he published as a verbatim record of the trial proceedings a few days after Turpin's execution. Our account of the trial depends heavily on this publication.

Proceedings were directed by the Counsel for the King, a position filled by Thomas Place, Recorder of York, whom we have already met taking care that Newcastle should be informed of Turpin's presence in York Castle as quickly as possible, and by Richard Crowle, who held this prestigious position through his locally powerful brother's influence. The accused in English criminal trials of the period had no right to legal representation, the theory being that the presiding judge looked after their interests as a sort of umpire between the prosecution and the accused. The first witness to be called against Turpin was Thomas Creasy, owner of the horses that Turpin stood charged for stealing. Creasy gave straightforward evidence about finding that his horses had gone, and told how he had found them through the help of his neighbour who picked up gossip in Brough after visiting Pocklington fair, and through the help of Richard Grassby. Creasy was able to give convincing evidence about the animals, claiming in particular that he was able to positively identify the mare, as he had bred her himself, and kept her for ten years. Turpin, asked at the end of Creasy's evidence if he had anything to ask the witness, made a complaint that he was to repeat several times in various forms that Thursday: 'I cannot say anything, for I have not any witnesses come this day, as I have expected, and therefore beg of your Lordship to put off my trial 'till another day.' He also claimed, bizarrely (and, given the inaccuracy in the dating of his alleged offences on his indictments, ironically), that he was in prison in York Castle on 18 August 1738, a notion that the King's Counsel immediately crushed.

The second witness was Captain Dawson, who gave evidence about buying the mare and the foal, and he was followed by Richard Grassby. Grassby gave evidence about the sale of the mare and foal, and also made a few points about Turpin's character: 'He had no settled way of living, that I know of at all, though a dealer, yet he was a stranger, and lived like a gentleman … he was reckoned a stranger.' George Goodyear, one of Thomas Creasy's neighbours, was called in and gave brief evidence about the mare and foal, and then Grassby was called upon again to confirm that Turpin had appeared with the suspect mare and foal in August.

The next two witnesses to be called were James Smith ('Mr James Smith' to the court, indicating a certain status) and Mr Edward Saward, 'who came from Essex by order of the justices of that county, were called to prove this Palmer to be Richard Turpin, the noted highwayman'. Smith, asked initially if he recognised Turpin, replied, 'Yes, I knew him at Hempstead in Essex where he was born, I knew him when he was a child', adding that 'I knew his father and all his relations, and he married one of my father's maids'. Smith gave more evidence in this vein, and also told the court of the discovery of the letter from Turpin to his brother-in-law. Turpin, asked if he had any questions to ask Smith, replied simply, 'I never knew him.' Edward Saward gave his evidence next. He comes across as a rather fussy man, and his habit of making statements 'upon my soul' evidently irritated the King's Counsel ('Friend, you have sworn once already, you need not swear again'). But his evidence constituted a useful supplement to James Smith's. Saward was also from Hempstead, had known Turpin for many years, and had bought 'a great many good joints of meat of him' after he had set up as a butcher, and was able to identify him positively as 'Dick Turpin, the son of John Turpin who keeps the Bell at Hempstead'. Turpin, so Kyll tells us, 'denied he knew Edward Saward but seemed at last to own [i.e. acknowledge] Smith'. James Smith was questioned further, and stated that when he first identified Turpin in York Castle the highwayman 'did confess to know me and said unto me two or three times, "Let us bung our eyes in drink", and I drank with him, which is this Richard Turpin'. The evidence of these Essex witnesses had no relevance to the charges of horse-theft on which Turpin was standing trial, but they were obviously useful in making much easier the court's task of holding Turpin should the charges of horse-theft fail.

Turpin was then questioned. He claimed that he bought the mare and foal from John Whitehead, who kept an inn near Heckington. He also repeated the story that he had changed his name to Palmer, which he claimed was his mother's maiden name (in fact, it was Parminter: was 'Palmer' a streamlined version of this, or a northern mishearing of Turpin's southern accent that he had decided to go along with?). He claimed that he had adopted the alias 'having been long out of trade, and run myself in debt'. Sir William Chapple gave his directions to the jury, and the jurymen 'without leaving court brought in their verdict "Guilty"'. The second charge, of stealing the gelding, engendered less lengthy proceedings. Creasy was called again, and gave a description of the horse and told how he had found it at an inn in Beverley. Carey Gill, the constable of Welton, told how he had arrested Turpin for shooting a cock, and how Turpin had ridden the gelding when he, Gill, had escorted him from Welton to Beverley House of Correction. Finally, Smith was called on again to confirm that John Palmer was, in fact, Richard Turpin, replying that 'I have known him from his infancy these twenty-two years; and he is the very Richard Turpin which I have known at Hempstead, the son of John Turpin of that town'. Turpin, asked if he had any more to say, simply replied, 'I bought this horse of Whitehead.' The jury again returned a verdict of guilty.

The judge then asked Turpin if he could give any reason why the sentence of death should not be pronounced upon him. Turpin returned to a theme on which he had harped throughout the trial, alleging that he had not been allowed sufficient time to prepare his defence. He had begged that the trial should be put off until another day after Thomas Creasy had given his initial evidence, and at a later point claimed that he had sent a special messenger for witnesses, and when it transpired that these had not arrived, Turpin claimed that he would have them tomorrow, adding, 'I am sure no man can say ill of me in Yorkshire.' He then claimed that he had three witnesses in court, but these did not appear when called, his claims being probably based on desperation. Told that he had no witnesses, Turpin tried another tactic, claiming that 'I thought I should have been removed to Essex for I did not expect to be tried in this country, therefore I could not prepare witnesses to my character'. And now, asked by Chapple for reasons he could give that he should not be executed, Turpin replied, 'It is very hard upon me, my Lord, because I was not prepar'd for my defence.' The judge, obviously unsympathetic, responded, 'Why was you not? You knew the time of the Assizes as well as any person here.' Turpin then returned to his other theme: 'Several persons who came to see me assured me that I should be removed to Essex to be tried there, for which reason I thought it needless to prepare witnesses for my defence.' The judge replied, 'Whoever told you so were highly to blame; and as your country has found you guilty of a crime worthy of death, it is my office to pronounce sentence against you.' And that sentence was, indeed, death.

So Turpin's body, after being cut down at three in the afternoon on the day of his execution — long enough after Turpin had thrown himself off the ladder to be certain that the life had gone out of it — was laid out in the Blue Boar in Castlegate, where it attracted considerable public attention. At ten the next morning, Sunday 8 April, the body was buried 'in a neat coffin in St George's churchyard, within Fishergate postern'. Turpin had spent his three pounds ten shillings well, for 'the grave was dug very deep, and the persons whom he appointed his mourners ... took all possible care to secure the body'. Their efforts were, however, nearly frustrated. The medical profession of eighteenth-century England had a need for cadavers for dissection classes, and the bodies of executed felons constituted a major source of supply. The College of Physicians in London had long since been granted the right to 'anatomise' the corpses of felons hanged in the capital, and some idea of the general attitude to such customs can be gained from an Act of 1752 which, intended as deterrent legislation, provided that the bodies of those convicted of wilful murder should as a matter of course be given to the surgeons for dissection. We have considerable evidence of the bodies of executed felons being sent for dissection, and of hostile popular reactions to this custom (which included rioting against it) for London, but little such evidence for the provinces. The fate of Turpin's corpse shows that parallel practices were known in York.

On the Tuesday following Turpin's burial, at three in the morning, so a contemporary pamphlet informs us,

> some persons were discover'd moving off the body, which they had taken up, and the mob having got scent where it was carried to, and supposing it was to be anatomized, went to a garden in which it was deposited, and brought away the body through the streets of the city, in a sort of triumph, almost naked, being only laid on a board cover'd with some straw, and carried on four men's shoulders, and buried in the same grave, having filled the coffin with slack'd [i.e.slaked] lime.

The York mob were as anxious as the London mob to guard the bodies of convicted criminals from dissection.

Further details about the incident are given by hitherto unacknowledged records in the York City Archives. This documentation, the record of a number of recognizances issued at the meeting of the City's Sessions of 4 May 1739, is not very detailed, yet it provides intriguing further information on the fate of Turpin's corpse. The key figure was Marmaduke Palms

(or Palmes) of the city of York, surgeon, who was bound over
to answer for 'causing to be taken up the body of Richard
Turpin out of his grave', Palms having been assisted by a
labourer, possibly a servant, named Richard Hogg. John
Hornby was apparently the leader of a mob that subsequently
riotously entered Palm's garden and took Turpin's body from a
'garden house' where it had been placed, others, notably a porter
named James Fentiman, also being involved. Hornby was then
arrested by John Hepworth, constable of St Bartholomew's
parish and a bricklayer by trade, and Christopher Jackson the
younger and John Flint were responsible for leading a riotous
assault on the constable and his assistants, which led to
Hornby's rescue. Most of those concerned were simply dis-
charged at subsequent sessions, although Richard Hogg was
fined twenty shillings.

A grave purporting to be Turpin's can be found in what
remains of St George's churchyard (the current St George's
Church, just across the road, is a Catholic institution built in
1848 for the numerous Irish immigrants who had found work in
York after the Famine). The churchyard is off York's main
tourist track, on the fringe of the council housing to the south of
Walmgate, adjacent to the Tramways Working Men's Club.
The grave is big, perhaps necessarily so, given the legend that
Black Bess is also buried there, and the inscription on the head-
stone is of a considerably later date than 1739, and, indeed,
appears to be of a considerably later date than the inscriptions
on any of the other tombstones there. None of these other
inscriptions refer to people buried before the early nineteenth
century. The closest grave to that supposedly occupied by
Turpin and Black Bess is that of Rebecca, the wife of John

Reynolds, who died in 1817. Others include those of Jane Baker, aged just seventeen but already married when she died in 1850, and John Carter ('A loving husband and a father dear, A faithful friend lies buried here'), who had at least reached the age of seventy-four before his demise in 1852.

Thus it is in the remnant of a graveyard in an undistinguished corner of a small provincial town that there is the last resting place of what is now a legendary figure, the only criminal of the many hundreds executed in eighteenth-century England whom the modern public still remembers. Most of those many hundreds were mundane thieves and burglars, essentially of the type with which we are so familiar today. Some, on the other hand, were representatives of the category of criminal that posterity has chosen to romanticise: highway robbers.

chapter *two*

HIGHWAYMEN

Let us begin with a visual image, one of those large and dramatic paintings that were so characteristic of the Victorian era. The central character is female, a young gentlewoman, attractive and dark haired, dressed fashionably and expensively in the style of the 1660s. Her gaze, apprehensive yet perhaps fascinated, is directed not at the viewer, but rather at a man who stands in front of her, his back to us and his face in half-profile as we look at the picture. He is also well dressed, with a frock-coat and thigh boots, with lace at his collar and cuffs, and his hat held in his left hand at waist height. He is about to dance, and is striking an elegant pose. Behind these two figures stands an immobile stagecoach, immobile because a highway robbery is taking place. The coachmen and other passengers are being robbed, some at gunpoint, by masked men, and an elderly man, again well dressed, sits to the left of the picture, his arms bound behind his back. Beside him stands one of the robbers, masked like his fellows, but, rather than menacing victims with his pistol, playing on a small, recorder-like wind instrument. The painting, which hangs in Manchester City Art Gallery, is entitled *Claude Duval*, and the artist responsible for it was one of the major painters of his day, William Powell Frith.

Frith, who is today perhaps best remembered for his panoramic and superbly detailed *Derby Day*, recalled in his autobiography that his inspiration for the painting came from an incident recounted in Chapter 3 of that early Victorian best-seller, Macaulay's *History of England*. Macaulay, referring to highwaymen in his vivid description of England around 1685, singled Claude Duval (of whom we shall hear more in a few pages) out for special attention, and recounted how on one occasion he 'stopped a lady's coach, in which there was a booty of four hundred pounds; how he took only one hundred, and suffered the fair owner to ransom the rest by dancing a coranto with him on the heath'. Frith, attracted by what he termed 'the dramatic character of the subject', researched his painting well, finding a suitable heath near Dorchester to use as the setting, obtaining from Lord Darnley of Chobham a vintage coach dating from the reign of Charles II to use as a model, and consulting a contemporary expert on historic clothing, William Frederick Fairholt, about his characters' dress. The painting took up much of the artist's energies during 1859, and on 31 December of that year he noted that he regarded it as 'the most successful picture of its class that I have ever done – better in art than "Derby Day"; but it will not be so popular by a long way'. Frith's estimates of the painting's future popularity proved correct, although the fact that the painting was purchased by an art dealer for £1,700 while it was still in progress probably provided adequate compensation. What is striking is that two hundred years after Duval flourished, and a generation after highway robbery had ceased to be a threat in England, Frith was able to represent the highwayman as a dashing, elegant, brave and gallant figure. And, a century and a half after Frith painted this work, that is still very much how we like to imagine our highwaymen.

So much for the image. For a flavour of the reality, let us turn to a highway robbery tried at the Essex assizes in March 1739, a few days before Dick Turpin stood trial and was convicted at York, the same sessions, in fact, where his father John Turpin escaped being tried for having stolen the horse Dick had left with him. The case involved a labourer named Daniel Saddler from Great Bentley who, according to his indictment,

> in the king's highway there with a certain offensive weapon called a hedge stake in and upon one Frances the wife of Thomas Maskall then & there in the peace of God and our said lord the king then & there being, unlawfully, malitiously, violently and feloniously did make an assault with an intent the goods, chattels and money of the said Thomas from the person and against the will of the said Frances then and there feloniously to steal, take and carry away.

No dancing of corantos or gallantry here, but rather a nasty robbery with violence which, along with an identical offence perpetrated on the same day against Mary, the wife of Joseph Wanklyn, led to Saddler being transported to the colonies. Criminals were no more romantic in the eighteenth century than they are today, and most highway robberies were perpetrated by the Daniel Saddlers of the period rather than by the gentleman highwaymen of our imaginings.

Surprisingly to the modern reader, there was, in fact, no

2. *A detail from John Haynes's* The South West Prospect of the City of York, *a print of 1731. Two men talk at the Southern tip of York racecourse. Beneath them, and badly out of scale, is the York gallows, the 'Three Legged Mare' upon which Turpin was executed (University of York Library).*

3. *The highwayman romanticized in high culture: William Powell Frith's* Claude Duval, *completed in 1860 (Manchester Art Gallery).*

separate legal offence of highway robbery, a point made neatly by Richard Burn in his much-reprinted manual for justices of the peace. After a discussion of the law relating to the maintenance of the highway, Burn simply wrote: 'Highwaymen. See Robbery'. The author of an earlier, and almost equally much reprinted handbook for justices, Michael Dalton, defined robbery thus:

> Robbery (in Latin *rapina*) is properly the felonious taking of any thing from the person of another, or in his presence, against his will, by assault in the high-way, or elsewhere, and putting him in fear thereby: and here, although the thing taken, be but to the value of one halfpenny, yet is it felony; for which the offender shall suffer death, without benefit of clergy. As if one by the high-way assaulteth me, and taketh away my purse, money, or other goods.

Dalton and Burn (who followed the earlier writer in this respect) agreed that the definition of 'highway' was a fairly wide one, including footpaths, or, indeed, as far as Burn was concerned, 'a river common to all men'.

But from the late Elizabethan period, when central government first started expressing its concerns about gangs of mounted robbers operating on the fringes of the capital, it was clear that highway robbery had entered both the public consciousness and the attitudes of law enforcement agencies as a distinct offence, and one of considerable seriousness. Indeed, the prevalence of highway robbery, much like that of street crime today, by the early eighteenth century came to serve contemporary opinion as a barometer for the general state of law and order. There was also a sense that, since the highway was the *king's* highway, robberies there offered a special affront to royal authority, and were a specially grievous burden on the king's loyal subjects as they went about their legitimate business. There were a number of proclamations and Acts against highwaymen over the seventeenth century, perhaps the most significant of these being the 'Highwayman Act' of 1693, which aimed to enhance the arrest rate for the offence by encouraging robbers to turn king's evidence against their associates, offering a pardon to those whose evidence led to the conviction of at least two of their accomplices. A fair proportion of highwaymen whose biographies are recorded in the literature of the period came to their end through this type of informing, or, indeed, at certain points in their career saved their own skins by turning their accomplices in. The Act, moreover, offered £40 to any member of the public who apprehended a highwayman who was subsequently convicted, and also made the horse, money, guns and other effects of a convicted highwayman the property of those who were responsible for his apprehension, provided that these goods were not themselves stolen in the first place.

Thus there was a fair degree of official concern about highway robbery, and, as Daniel Saddler's indictment suggests, cases of highway robbery were regularly tried before the criminal courts. In Essex, for example, surviving documentation shows that between 1620 and 1680 seventy-nine highway robberies, involving one hundred and nine accused, all male, were tried at the county assizes. Thirty-eight of these were hanged. The offences, as might be expected, were clustered around the London peripheries, the very area where Dick Turpin was to commence his criminal career in the next century. The robbers varied: the famous Claude Duval was among those indicted, but most of those coming before the Essex authorities were less imposing figures. One Essex justice of the peace noted early in the 1680s how a Mr Riman complained that

> about one of the clocke this morning Peter Hall (in company with four men more) did in the rode [road] in the parish of West Ham tooke hould of his horse's bridell he beinge upon his backe and did bid him stand, upon which Mr Riman quitted his horse and tooke hould of the said Peter Hall (the others running away) and carryed him to the constable who brought him hither.

Peter Hall and his associates were clearly not very impressive criminals, and his case reinforces the suspicion that the majority of those tried before the Essex assizes in our sample were far distant from the silk-clad and audacious highwayman of later myth. Certainly the value of the goods allegedly stolen would support this contention, with fifteen of the indictments being brought for our sample of Essex robberies worth less than a pound. There is scattered evidence of these highway robbers offering violence to their victims, and one case, in 1668, of a victim of highway robbery being murdered, but in general the impression of the offence formed by the court records is more low key than might have been expected.

A similar impression is created by a highway robbery's position in a much larger sample of criminal cases, those tried in Surrey from 1660 to 1800. If by the early eighteenth century evidence exists for the type of romantic gentleman highwayman of tradition, it is nevertheless clear that many of the highway robberies that were indicted at that time were carried out by men of low status and on foot, and that it is the menace and brutality of these robberies which is the most marked feature of such qualitative evidence about them as we have. The total of robberies was small when compared to larceny and burglary, and the value of the goods stolen was, if greater than that in most larceny cases, usually not massive. As might be deduced from this, many of the victims of robbers, highwaymen and footpads alike, were poor: they included pedlars, people out buying provisions, men going to work, or even a 'poor milk woman': there was little of the spirit of Robin Hood about these offences. Again, highway robberies tended to be clustered around the London peripheries, with a massive concentration in Southwark, but with lesser clusters (and these more likely to be highway robbery as understood today) occurring in Putney, Wimbledon, Kingston, Croydon, and Egham, where Bagshot Heath provided helpful terrain for those wanting to rob travellers on the main road to the south-west.

So much for the evidence of bodies of court records. But it is not to the careful scrutiny of this documentation that we owe our image of the highwayman. This originates in the printed biographies of such offenders that were becoming increasingly common by the end of the seventeenth century. These, naturally enough, tended to focus on the more notorious highwaymen, those who had enjoyed an exceptionally long career, or whose crimes were seen as especially daring and newsworthy. But, if we are considering where our modern image of the highwayman comes from, it is to these accounts of their lives that we must turn. Perhaps the most remarkable of these sometimes much-reprinted criminal biographies was that of William

Davis, 'The Golden Farmer', who had robbed on the highway for over forty years before he was executed and his body hanged in chains on Bagshot Heath in December 1689. Another highwayman with a lengthy career was William Page, executed in 1758. Page led a varied early life, being for some time a member of a company of strolling players that he had joined after meeting them at York, and from which he was dismissed after being drunk on stage during a performance at Scarborough. Disappointed in this career, he turned highwayman and carried out three hundred robberies before his execution. Others achieved fame through large-scale crimes, like Thomas Rowland, who crowned a career of eighteen years as a highwayman by carrying out a robbery worth £1,200 on Hounslow Heath in 1699, for which he was apprehended and executed. Against such imposing criminals, however, must be set the somewhat pathetic figure of Thomas Barkwith, an 'unfortunate young gentleman' and an accomplished scholar and linguist, who fell into debt, and was executed in December 1739 after committing his first and only highway robbery.

Constructing a social profile of this sample of highwaymen memorable enough to be celebrated by contemporary hack writers is fairly straightforward. For the most part they were drawn from what historians now term the middling sort, respectable and often substantial tradesmen and farmers. Their short biographies almost invariably refer to their solid family backgrounds, their parents being variously referred to as 'honest', 'very reputable', 'honest and comfortable', or 'creditable'. Highway robbers included men who had served their apprenticeships as butcher, bricklayer, shoemaker, baker, or tailor, and men who, as apprentices, had absconded from bakers, tanners, upholsterers, shoemakers, and an attorney at law, or who had been gentle-men's servants but had been dismissed for pilfering. Some were tradesmen who had fallen on hard times through no fault of their own, like Ned Bonnet, a Cambridgeshire grocer who had once been worth £600, but who had turned to highway rob-bery after losing everything in a fire. More commonly, however, the short accounts of their lives record that they fell into tempta-tion, or had an entrenched inclination to idleness and delin-quency, thus allowing the deployment of that familiar morality tale in which small offences in youth led inexorably to those more serious offences for which they suffered death on the gal-lows. The roll-call of notorious highwaymen included a few fairly elderly individuals, perhaps the most remarkable being William Davis, aged sixty-four when he was hanged. But, typi-cally, they were, like Turpin, in their late twenties or early thir-ties when the law caught up with them. And they were more likely than the average male population to have seen military service: to take just a few examples, Patrick O'Bryan served in the Coldstream Guards, Jack Bird served in the foot guards and saw service at the siege of Maastricht in the late seventeenth cen-tury, Will Hollyday served under William III in Flanders in the same period, apparently committing a good number of rob-beries there, and Jack Withrington served in the Earl of Oxford's regiment of horse.

Despite the claims of many highwaymen, of some of their contemporaries, and of many later popular historians, highway robbers included in their number very few gentlemen in the true seventeenth- or eighteenth-century meaning of the term. Sir Simon Clarke, baronet, along with Lieutenant Robert Arnott were tried and convicted as highwaymen in 1731, Clarke having

the highest social rank of anybody to suffer this fate. Instruc-
tively, after he had made 'a most pathetic and moving speech,
which had such an effect, that there was scarce a dry eye in the
house', the court 'considering the antiquity, worth and dignity
of Sir Simon's ancestors, the services they had done their king
and country, together with the youth and melancholy circumstances of the unhappy gentlemen', recommended that the pair
should be reprieved. There were, perhaps, a few younger sons of
the gentry who drifted into highway robbery, one such being
Tom Cox, youngest son of a gentleman from Blandford in
Dorset, executed in June 1691 at the age of twenty-six after a
number of robberies, Charles II's former court jester being
among his victims. But one suspects that many of those highwaymen who claimed and were afforded gentlemanly status
were at best on the fringes of gentility. One such was James
MacLaine (there are numerous variant spellings of his name),
'The Gentleman Highwayman', executed at Tyburn in October 1750. MacLaine was a clergyman's son (MacLaine's
brother also followed this profession), and his claims to real gentility were largely aspirational: as the author of his first, and
largely sympathetic, biography commented acidly, 'in short, he
had a passion for nothing but fine cloaths [clothes] and a rich
wife'.

The claims to gentility that highwaymen sometimes made,
or which were made on their behalf, were also obviated by their
tendency to commit very unpleasant crimes. Patrick O'Bryan,
the former Coldstream Guardsman, with four accomplices carried out a robbery on the house of Lancelot Wilmot in Wiltshire that was very much in the style of the house-robberies
which were to be committed a generation later by Dick Turpin

and his associates in the Essex gang. They tied up three servants, Wilmot and his wife, gang-raped his daughter, rifled the house and took goods worth £2,500, and on their departure set the building on fire, with fatal results for the three servants. Tom Jones, after a lengthy career of robbery, was hanged at Launceston in 1702 after he robbed and then raped a farmer's wife. A young man named Raby, an accomplice of famous robber William Udall, whose life story reads like a prototype for Hogarth's idle apprentice, cut off the finger of a woman in order to steal a ring she was unwilling to relinquish. Another woman, in this case a pedlar, who in 1722 declared that she knew the identity of three highwaymen she saw robbing a stagecoach, had her tongue cut out by them. Jack Blewit, after a remarkable life that included being the slave of African kings, was executed in 1713 for shooting a farmer's daughter through the head and robbing her of fourteen pounds. And, perhaps more understandably, many highwaymen had no compunction about shooting people who recognised them, or who were trying to arrest them. Patrick O'Bryan was one of the 'half hanged', having been secretly revived after his body had been cut down from the gallows at Gloucester. A little later he met the man whose evidence had led to his conviction on that occasion, and shot him. William Udall shot a coachman who resisted him, and Jack Shrimpton shot the constable who tried to arrest him when he was discovered in a Bristol bawdy house in 1713. Violence is a theme that is rarely absent from these highwaymen's biographies.

And, as the biographies of Turpin and many other of the 'notorious' highwaymen demonstrate, those we think of as highway robbers frequently were, or had been, involved in other types of crime that lacked highway robbery's romantic cachet.

William Udall began his criminal career while still an apprentice, consorting with 'a number of young pickpockets, with whom he used to go out of an evening and steal watches, swords, hats and anything they could lay their hands on', and towards the end of his career was involved in those street robberies that the highwayman was meant to despise. Jacob Halsey, 'The Quaker Highwayman', hanged at Maidstone in 1691, similarly began his criminal activities as a member of a gang of thieves, pickpockets and card sharps. Tim Buckley, executed in 1701, was also a house-breaker and street robber, on one occasion robbing and subsequently raping at gun-point the wife of a constable who had previously arrested him. Henry Cook, who committed many robberies, especially in Essex, in the years immediately after Turpin's death, was also a horse-thief. Overall, it is clear that most highwaymen, particularly those based in the London area, were firmly locked into the unglamorous world of pickpocketing, street robbery, burglary, prostitution, and the fencing of stolen goods, all of these facets of the well-developed criminal underworld in the capital. Thus the modern observer is left wondering how, why and when the highwayman was selected as the romantic figure of later, and to some extent seventeenth- and eighteenth-century, legend.

For clues towards the answer to this question, let us turn to the careers of two extremely famous highwaymen: James Hind and, to return to the subject of Frith's painting, Claude Duval.

James Hind, or Captain James Hind as the reports describing

the event referred to him, was executed on 24 September 1652. He had been apprehended some time before, betrayed by a close friend while he had been in hiding in the Fleet Street area of London. He was examined, and then committed to Newgate, and was indicted for several offences at the Old Bailey on 12 December 1651. No capital offence could be proved against him, and he was therefore taken down to Reading, and indicted for having committed a murder in Berkshire. He was found guilty of manslaughter, an offence that sometimes, albeit infrequently, led to hanging, but was saved, and the authorities thwarted, by a general act of oblivion and pardon being passed the day after his trial. But they were determined to get Hind, and by an Order of Council he was removed on a writ of habeas corpus to be tried for treason. For Hind was that rarest of entities, a politically motivated highwayman. Civil war between king and parliament had broken out in England in 1642, and in 1649 the victory of parliament, or perhaps more accurately of a hardline military faction and their civilian adherents, had led to the execution of Charles I. His son, the future Charles II, had attempted to lead a royalist rising in 1651, the enterprise having been smashed at the Battle of Worcester in September of that year. James Hind was one of those who had offered Charles Stuart active assistance, and it was for this that he was sentenced to death At the place of execution he assured his listeners that most of the robberies he committed had parliamentarians as their victims, and that nothing troubled him so much as dying before his royal master was back on the throne, adding that the members of the parliamentarian regime were a rebellious and disloyal crew who deserved execution much more than he did. And then Hind, as a convicted traitor, was subjected to the bar-

barities of hanging, drawing and quartering. He was hanged briefly, cut down while still conscious, castrated and disembow-elled while still alive, his genitals and intestines being burnt on the gallows in his sight, and then beheaded, his body quartered, the head and four sections of his body then being boiled in tar for preservation and exhibited around Worcester as a grim reminder of the virtues of obedience to the new government.

There was little in Hind's early life to suggest that he would come to such an end. He was born at Chipping Norton in Oxfordshire, the only son of an honest and religious father. The family was apparently reasonably well off, and the young James was sent to school until he was fifteen, by which time he was fully literate and had a good knowledge of arithmetic. His schooling over, he was apprenticed to a butcher in Chipping Norton, but according to the accounts of his life his master was a very difficult man, and James, supplied with money by his mother, broke his service and ran away to London. There, like so many other highwaymen whose biographies have come down to us, Hind developed a taste for pleasure, fell into bad company, and then turned to crime to support his newly acquired lifestyle. Apprehended in the company of a prostitute who had just picked a gentleman's pocket, Hind was committed to one of London's minor prisons, the Poultry Compter, and held overnight. He was released the next morning, there being no evidence against him, but during his brief incarceration had made the acquaintance of somebody else who was being held on suspicion, an experienced highwayman named Thomas Allen. The two men went for a drink together after being released, struck up a friendship, and shortly afterwards began robbing on the highway together, their first robbery taking place on one of the favoured locations for such exploits, Shooters Hill on the Kentish peripheries of the metropolitan area.

The beginning of their criminal career roughly coincided with the execution of Charles I, and, according to the stories of Hind's exploits that were printed subsequently, the two men decided to be totally unsparing of parliamentarians. They attempted to hold up a coach containing Oliver Cromwell, but he was too heavily guarded: Hind only escaped with great difficulty, killing his horse in the process, and Allen was captured and subsequently executed. According to the accounts of his life, Hind's later victims, as well as the usual run of unfortunate gentleman and tradesmen, included Hugh Peters the regicide, John Bradshaw, who had presided over the court that had tried Charles I and passed the death sentence on him, and another regicide, Colonel Thomas Harrison. The modern reader might be pardoned for a slight scepticism about one highwayman's chances of meeting and successfully robbing three such eminent members of the parliamentarian regime, but Hind's hostility to the parliamentarian and republican causes was to become an essential part of his later legend.

And this legend was to become unusually potent and long-lasting. His apprehension in late 1651 was accompanied by a flurry of publications, his capture even being noted in a parliamentary newspaper, the *Weekly Intelligencer of the Commonwealth* for 11–18 November 1651. There were a number of descriptions of his conduct and his declarations to the court in the early stages of his incarceration, these generally being couched in very favourable terms. He was pressured to seek pardon and turn evidence against his previous accomplices, but he stoutly refused to do this, and it was reported that at his Old Bailey trial 'while he was at the bar, he deported himself with undanted [sic] courage, yet with a civill behaviour, and smiling countenance'. But the apprehension of Hind was to see something new. The trial of an individual highwayman had been made the subject of pamphlets before, but Hind's arrest was followed by a flurry of publications that aimed to furnish the reader with brief accounts of his exploits clearly intended to entertain rather than edify. One of the more serious publications, *The Declaration of Captain Hind*, deplored the appearance of 'sundry and various relations of the proceedings of Capt. James Hind, fraught with impertinent stories, and new invented fictions', but the success of such chapbooks as *A Pill to Purge Melancholy: or, merry Newes from Newgate, wherein is set forth the pleasant Jests, witty Conceits, and excellent Couzenages of Captain James Hind and his Associates* demonstrated a taste for 'impertinent stories, and new invented fictions' among the reading public. The highwayman story as a source of entertainment had arrived.

And, in Hind's case, it was to stay. Charles Johnson, author of a compendium of the lives of the most famous highwaymen, murderers, street-robbers, and pirates, published in 1734, described Hind as 'a man as much talk'd of to this day as almost any of his profession that ever lived, and who was as distinguished by his pleasantry in all his adventures', adding that 'he never in his life robbed a man, but at the same time said or did something diverting'. His memory was kept alive by the prominent place he enjoyed in the collections of lives of highwaymen that began to appear from the early eighteenth century onwards, and by more popular works. Thus a chapbook entitled *No Jest like a true Jest: being a compendious Record of the merry Life and maddest Exploits of Capt. James Hind, the greatest Robber of England,* originating from the popular works that came into print at the time of his execution, was reprinted in 1750, 1765, 1775, 1805 and 1817. Well into the eighteenth century, Hind's reputation was helped by his adherence to the royalist cause. The animosities unleashed in the Civil Wars and their aftermath took two or three generations to work themselves out, and an anti-parliamentarian highwayman stood an enhanced chance of receiving a good press, and entering popular consciousness. But, from the start, Hind was also acquiring some peculiar attributes. *The Declaration of Captain Hind* has him claiming that he never shed a drop of blood, and that 'neither did I ever take the worth of a penny from a poor man'. In the early eighteenth century Hind was remembered as a man 'celebrated for his generosity to all sorts of people, more especially to his kindness to the poor, which is reported was so extraordinary, that he never injured the property of any person who had not a complete share of riches', while by that time Hind's unwillingness to shed blood was also an established component of his legend.

According to the accounts of his life, Hind's criminal career and his eventual demise were very much shaped by the peculiar contingency of his having lived through the 1640s and early 1650s. In much the same way, the life and later legend of the subject of our second analysis, Claude Duval, who made another contribution to the formation of the highwayman myth, owed much to the next episode in English history, the Restoration. Duval (his surname is another that appears in several forms) was a Frenchman, born in Domfront in Normandy. At the age of thirteen or fourteen his parents (his father was a miller) sent him out into the world to seek his fortune. Accordingly, Duval went to the regional capital, Rouen, was hired to help ride post horses back to Paris, and at the same time made the acquaintance of some English gentlemen. These seem to have more or less adopted the youth, and on arrival at Paris he lodged near them in the Faubourg St Germain, at that time an area heavily populated by English *émigrés*, most of them royalists who were in exile during the ascendancy of Cromwell. Duval generally made himself useful to the English *émigré* community, running errands for them and picking up odd jobs at a house called the St Esprit in the Rue de Bourchière, an establishment that combined the functions of a cook-shop, brothel, and ale-house. He obviously attracted a patron from among the English in exile, and when the Restoration of Charles II came in 1660 Duval came to England as the footman of a person of quality.

Duval, like so many of the highwaymen whose lives were recorded in any sort of detail, became addicted to drunkenness, whoring and gambling, and, finding himself in need of cash to support these activities, turned to highway robbery. He rapidly achieved a considerable notoriety for his activities as a highway-man, and apparently was the first named in a proclamation for the apprehending of several notorious highwaymen issued shortly after he began his activities. He continued to rob on the road, but returned to France for a while when things became too hot in England. When he ran short of money he continued to live by sharp practices there; one story told of that period of his life was that he tricked a Jesuit confessor of Louis XIV with a scam involving pretended alchemy, and then robbed him. He soon returned to England, and resumed robbing on the highways. The exact story of his downfall remains uncertain, although it is gen-erally agreed that he was taken while drunk at an inn called the Hole-in-the-Wall in Chandos Street in London, after which he was committed to Newgate, convicted, sentenced to death, and executed on 21 January 1670. Although his demise did not cause the same literary stir as did that of James Hind, his apprehension and execution was commemorated in print, notably by the anonymous *Mémoires of Monsieur du Vall: containing the History of his Life and Death*, which was constantly pirated by those writing later biographies of this most remarkable of highwaymen.

If the legend built around Hind opened up the possibility that the highwayman's life might serve as a source of entertainment, Duval's legend established the highwayman as a romantic, swashbuckling daredevil. Above all, Duval had a reputation as a ladies' man. One story, contained in the *Mémoires* of 1670, repeated in all of the later accounts of Duval's life, and, indeed, serving as a source of inspiration for Frith's painting, illustrates this point, and serves as a prototype for many later real-life occurrences, and even more later fictional constructions, of acts of gallantry by highwaymen. Apparently Duval received information that a knight and his wife were travelling with £400 in a coach, and he led five associates to intercept them. The couple realised that they were being overtaken by highwaymen, and the lady, 'a young sprightly creature', took out a flageolet and began to play it, whereupon Duval took out a flageolet of his own, which he had about his person (again, the sceptical reader might regard this as something of an odd coincidence), and rode up to the coach playing it. The coach had halted by now, and Duval complimented the knight on his wife's musical ability, opined that she could dance as well as she could play, and asked him if indeed she would dance with him. The knight agreed, and immediately the footman opens the door and the knight comes out; Du Vall leaps lightly off his horse and hands the lady down. It was surprising to see how gracefully he moved upon the grass; scarce a dancing-master in London but would have been as proud to have shown such ability in a pair of pumps as Du Vall showed in a great pair of French riding-boots. As soon as the dance was over he waits of the lady back to the coach, without offering her the least affront.

Duval then pointed out to the lady's husband that he had not paid for the music, and was given a hundred pounds, whereupon the highwayman, who knew the real extent of the wealth being carried in the coach, told the knight that 'your noble behaviour has excused you the other three hundred which you have in the coach with you'.

Duval's reputation among the ladies for dash and gallantry was demonstrated, on the strength of the 1670 *Mémoires*, and later accounts, by their reactions to his trial and execution. 'There were a great company of ladies', we are informed, 'and those not of the meanest degree, visited him in prison, and interceded for his pardon.' Their intercessions were in vain, for Duval went to the gallows, where his last moments were witnessed by many ladies of quality, tearful under their vizards. After he was hanged his corpse was taken to the Tangier tavern in St Giles, where he lay in state all night in a room hung in black cloth, in which eight wax tapers were burning, and eight 'tall gentleman' stood in attendance with long cloaks. The author of the *Mémoires* noted that 'this story of lying in state seem'd so improbable, and such an audacious mocquerie of the laws', that he only came to believe it after 'I had it again, and again from several gentlemen who had the curiosity to see him'. After his death a manuscript speech was found in Duval's clothing in which he paid fulsome compliments to the women of England, while apparently when he was buried in Covent Garden church there were many women among his mourners. A white marble stone was laid over him, with a verse epigraph, part of which supposedly ran:

Here lies Du Vall, reader, if male thou art,
Look to thye purse; if female, to thy heart.
Much havoc hath he made of both; for all
Men he made stand, and women he made fall.

Duval possibly more than any other of his profession established the image of the highwayman which was to prove so resilient in later generations.

This was not the only verse that commemorated Duval's death. Samuel Butler wrote a Pindaric ode in the recently deceased highwayman's honour. The last two verses of this dwelt on his attractiveness to women, although earlier in the piece Butler developed the conceit that Duval was like a general laying siege to London, whose operations prevented supplies of foodstuffs from reaching the city. Much the same point was made by the author of another piece published at the time of Duval's fall in 1670, a rather pedestrian criminal biography that commented on the complaints that the 'poor market folks' made about the impact of Duval's activities on their trade. Yet it was his gallantry for which he was best remembered. As the author of the *Mémoires*, dwelling upon the flageolet-playing and dancing incident, put it:

He evidenced his skill in instrumental musick, by playing on his flageolet; in vocal by his singing; for (as I should have told you before) there being no violins, du Vall sung the corant himself. He manifested his agility of body, by lightly dismounting off his horse, and with ease and freedome getting up again, when he took his leave, his excellent deportment, by his incomparable dancing, and his graceful manner of taking the hundred pound, his generosity in taking no more, his wit and eloquence, and readiness at repartees in the whole discourse with the knight and the lady, the greatest part of which I have been forced to omit.

With Duval, the idea of what a highwayman might be like took on a whole new dimension. Clearly, he might now demonstrate the polite gentlemanly standards that the ever more ornate culture of Restoration England regarded as desirable. It is no accident that the author of the *Mémoires*, while helping create this image, should, in his 'Apology' at the end of the piece, express his regret at the spreading influence of French fashions and cultural norms, which he clearly regarded as adding an unnecessary level of ornateness to everyday social interactions, including, it would seem, highway robbery.

Yet there was one story, current in 1670 and repeated in the later accounts of Duval's life, which shows even this most dashing, gallant and genteel of highwaymen in a bad light. Duval on one occasion was seeking victims on Blackheath, and came across a coach filled with 'ladies of quality', among whom was a child with a silver sucking-bottle. On this occasion Duval robbed them roughly, taking money, watches, rings, and even the child's sucking-bottle. Neither the infant's tears nor the ladies' pleas would make him restore it, until one of his companions forced him to give it back. Our 1670 author admitted that this episode appeared to 'seem to his disadvantage', although he also declared that 'I shall seek to make no reflection upon this story, both because I do not design to render him odious, or make this pamphlet more prolix'. For a highwayman to steal a child's feeding-bottle was beyond the pale: it is equally clear that Duval himself seems to have seen no problem with so doing.

So, by the turn of the seventeenth and eighteenth centuries, the doings of highwaymen regularly figured in pamphlets and chapbooks, most of the more memorable highwaymen might expect a pamphlet or two to be published at the time of their execution, while the apprehension and execution of the really notorious robber, like James Hind, might result in a number of publications and the beginnings of what was to become a long-lasting legend. But in 1714 there came something new. That year was to see the publication of the first edition of Captain Alexander Smith's *The History of the Lives of the most noted Highway-Men, Foot-Pads, Housebreakers, Shop-Lifts and Cheats of both Sexes, in and about London, and in other Places in Great Britain, for above forty Years Past*. Little is known of Smith apart from his publications. His *History of the Lives* was followed by a series of publications under his name, all of them dealing with the seamier aspects of early eighteenth-century life. There was a supplement of 1720, which contained a 'Thieves' Grammar', and the 'Secret History of the most celebrated Beau[ties] of Quality, and Jilts, from Fair Rosamund down to [...]. The 'Thieves' Grammar' was related to the *Thieves ne[w ...ing] Dictionary or the Words, Proverbs, Terms and Phrases used in the Language of Thieves* that Smith published in 1719, while in 1716 he had already published his *Court of Venus, or Cupid restored to Sight*. One of his best-selling works was a tract sold for a shilling entitled *The comical and tragical History of the Lives and Adventures of the most noted Bayliffs in and about London and Westminster* of 1723, a work that enjoyed commercial success, as a nineteenth-century commentator was to put it, 'mainly on account of the coarseness of the drolleries', while he was also to publish a memoir of the life of Jonathan Wild, and *Court Intrigue, or an Account of the secret Mémoires of the British Nobility and Others*, this, his last known publication, coming in 1730.

Smith was clearly a prolific and successful writer, and a close analysis of his output would provide some interesting insights into the taste of the British reading public in the reigns of the first two Georges. But it is his *History of the Lives* for which he is now mainly remembered. This work, already an expensive collector's item in the late Victorian era, went through a number of editions, and clearly enjoyed a wide readership.

The taste of this readership for the lives of criminals proved to be long lasting. Smith's *History of the Lives* was followed in 1734 by the publication of another large compendium of criminal histories, Captain Charles Johnson's *A General History of the Lives and Adventures of the most famous Highwaymen, Murderers, Street-Robbers, &c, to which is added a genuine Account of the Voyages and Plunders of the most notorious Pirates*. Other such compendia, all of them more or less plagiarising similar works that had gone before, were published over the eighteenth century, perhaps the last in the series being the anonymous *Anecdotes, Bon Mots, Traits, Stratagems and Biographical Sketches of the most remarkable Highwaymen, Swindlers, and other daring Adventurers who have flourished, from a very early Period, to the present Time*, which appeared in 1797. And another printed source providing information about criminals for both contemporary readers and later historians was also responding to new demands. Since the later seventeenth century, details of criminal proceedings at the Old Bailey had been printed in a series of publications known to modern historians as *The Old Bailey Sessions Papers*. From about 1729 these accounts became fuller, and by the 1740s they provided extensive narratives of the lives and misdeeds of those hanged at Tyburn. There was evidently a constantly expanding market for printed criminal biographies, in much the same way as our current taste for television crime series seems insatiable.

The authors of these biographies, certainly those responsible for the large collections of them, were, as might have been anticipated, insistent that their writings served an important moral and didactic purpose. Smith stressed to need 'to recount the actions of criminal and wicked persons, that by the dreadful aspects of vice' others might 'be deterr'd from embracing her illusions', and by 1797 it was possible to declare 'that in every work which has hitherto been published on the present subject, the utility of recording examples to offended justice, has been earnestly enforced: and all possible objections to this kind of understanding have been ably answered'. There was also a tendency to stress the veracity of the stories that were offered up to the reading public. Smith was insistent that his narratives were 'the most unaccountable relations of irregular actions as ever were heard; penn'd all from their own mouths', and that 'we have been at no small pains to collect the lives of these wretches, being very punctual not only in decyphering their canting language, but also in divulging their covert engagements, cunning flatteries, treacherous compositions, and underhand compliances'.

The claims to higher moral purpose, and even to factual accuracy, ring hollow when the main function of these accounts was to entertain, and to meet a perceived public taste for sensationalised and semi-fictionalised accounts of the doings of notorious criminals. The narratives of the lives of highwaymen and other perpetrators of serious crime were usually devoid of much by way of moral comment (except, of course, when the story comes to the offender's apprehension and death) and, indeed, frequently have little by way of narrative structure. Story-telling techniques had advanced since the days of the Hind pamphlets in 1652, but to the modern reader the accounts of highwaymen's doings given, for example, by Smith and Johnson seem very much like a string of unconnected, indeed interchangeable, anecdotes that sometimes proceed through an incoherent story-line. And there is little by way of characterisation. We rarely get much more than a very obvious impression of the highwayman's motivation, and little by way of an impression of his psychological state. The highwayman of the eighteenth-century anthologies of criminal biographies is in many respects little more than a cardboard figure committing assorted crimes, and eventually reinforcing conventional morality by coming to his end at Tyburn or a provincial assize town.

Yet it is not quite as simple as that. The highwayman stories were frequently used to question the morality of the world in

which they were set. 'Doubtless it must make some of our readers merry', wrote Charles Johnson in 1734, 'when they observe
how often the heros of these sheets are introduced as talking of
conscience, virtue, honour, generosity, &c.' Perhaps he was
right: but as the first performance and lasting popularity of John
Gay's *Beggar's Opera* in 1728 reminds us, there existed a potential
for finding parallels between the doings of serious property
offenders and some of the representatives of 'straight' society.
Gay's most famous work operated on a variety of levels, and one
of its author's main objectives was to burlesque several of the
theatrical fashions of the period, not least the Italian style of
opera. Moreover, perhaps the most striking aspect of the opera is
the way in which it demonstrates how the motif of crime in general and highwaymen in particular had become powerful
enough to serve as a vehicle for social satire. Yet the targets for
satire were there, and many contemporaries must have sensed the
fit between the world of John Gay's highwaymen, fences and
prostitutes, and that of Sir Robert Walpole's political regime.

More generally, from the mid seventeenth century England
was becoming increasingly commercialised, a development that
has led some historians to claim that by the years around 1700
England was well on the way to becoming the world's first consumer society. At the very least, commerce and capitalism were
advancing rapidly, not always to the taste of more traditionally
minded observers. It is possible to see the highwayman,
upwardly mobile, ruthless and heavily profit-oriented, as
strongly representative of the new capitalism. But the tendency
of the criminal biographies of the period was to take a different
tack, and to develop a limited sympathy for lawbreakers who
were so frequently represented as robbing people who had made

money from their fellow men. Hence, to return to Johnson's words, 'conscience, virtue, honour, generosity, &c' in the highwayman could be contrasted with the morality of putting the pursuit of profit above honour and friendship. The politicisation of English society from the late seventeenth century added an additional facet. Hind could be presented both in his lifetime and subsequently as a royalist highwayman, and there is a sense that many other highwaymen of the 1650s showed royalist tendencies, while those of the next century frequently showed Jacobite, or at least Tory, ones, their preferred victims (on the strength of the tales told about them) being rich tradesmen, merchants, professionals (notably lawyers and clergymen), courtiers and politicians. Too much should not be made of this because these are the constructions of a semi-fictionalised, and possibly ideologically driven, image rather than reality. But the Whigs, on occasion, rose to the bait: 'all the rogues, whores, pimps, thieves, fools, and scoundrels in the kingdom', declared one Whig newspaper, were Tories. Conversely, the highwayman, preying on representatives of new commercial wealth, and on those who had done well out of the Glorious Revolution of 1688–9, could be presented as an ally, albeit a risky and ambivalent one, of traditional, backwoods Tory virtues.

Beneath all this there lay the growing acceptance of the notion that the highwayman was somehow a superior sort of criminal. The reality of highway robbery and of the people committing it cast severe doubts on this notion, yet it was one that became ever more strongly established as the eighteenth century progressed. The highwayman was presented as being nicer than the normal run of property offenders, footpads, burglars, common thieves, and so on. Although one doubts if this was the case of all of those accused of highway robbery, it was perhaps true of that select sample of highway robbers who were commemorated in the criminal biographies. The proportion of gentlemen among highway robbers was small, but there was a sprinkling, while a solid minority of notorious highwaymen had once been relatively prosperous tradesmen, at least some of whom, on appropriate occasions, were willing and able to ape the ways of their gentry betters. Unlike other property offenders, the highway robber showed what might be regarded as desirable attributes: horsemanship, daring and skill with weapons. Moreover, although in reality most highwaymen tended to operate in gangs, the criminal biographies enhanced the image of the daring and courageous highwayman by frequently having their subjects act alone.

All of these highwaymen's biographies open up windows on the world in which they lived, and indeed a few touch on the broad themes of global capitalism and the early stages of Empire. Let us return to Jack Blewit, who, as we have seen, was executed in 1713 after murdering a farmer's wife he had robbed. Blewit was born in a court off the Strand in London, the son of a shoemaker, and was apprenticed into that trade. But his father died when Blewit was still an apprentice, his mother could not control him, and, like so many others, he fell into a life of vice. He joined the army under James II, but when his regiment was disbanded on the removal of that monarch in 1688, he became a crew member on a slave ship. The ship sailed into the Gulf of Guinea, heading for 'Old Calabar' (the modern Calabar in Nigeria) and the Cross River Estuary, at that time a major centre for slave-trading. The ship loaded its cargo of black Africans, and Blewit and some other sailors were sent ashore to sell some remaining bars of copper, presumably the currency with which the slaves had been bought. Blewit was captured by natives, and was himself sold into slavery, serving successively with two tribal kings. He struck up a friendly relationship with the second of these, who agreed to sell him back to his countrymen if any came into the area and if a suitable price could be arranged. In due course another English ship put in to pick up slaves, and Blewit, after fourteen months of servitude, was redeemed for five bars of iron. This experience left him with an understandable disinclination for further seafaring, and on returning to England he decided to set up as a highwayman. He stole a horse at Marylebone, sold it to buy a saddle, pistols and other accoutrements, and then stole another horse, for which theft he was arrested, convicted and subsequently pardoned. Undeterred by the failure of this early attempt at crime, on his release Blewit set up as a footpad, robbed a gentleman, then killed his victim, managing to pass this off as an accidental death, and set himself up as a highwayman on the proceeds of this robbery. He was forty-five years old when he was eventually executed.

Blewit, despite the intrinsic interest of his career, does not come across as a romantic or dashing figure. But other stories showed highwaymen behaving with gallantry. One such was Jack Ovet, executed at Leicester in 1708. According to his much republished life story, on one occasion Ovet was robbing a gentleman when his victim told him that if Ovet had not come on him unexpectedly and surprised him, he would have had considerable trouble in parting him from his money. Ovet took up this challenge, and the two fought with their swords, eventually with fatal results for the gentleman. Many highwayman were also portrayed as offering pleasantries to, and indeed performing acts of gallantry for, the ladies they had set out to rob – Jack Ovet, for example, falling helplessly in love with a woman he encountered when he held up the Worcester stage coach. The tradition begun by Duval was to flourish during the century after his death. And there were also signs of an embryonic Robin Hood tradition developing around highwaymen. Evan Evans, out robbing with his brother William, came across a body of constables who were conveying about thirty men who had been 'pressed' (i.e. recruited for military or naval service) to Portsmouth. The two brothers attacked the constables, tied them up, robbed them and let the thirty pressed men go free. Benjamin Child, possibly the most famous highwayman of his day and one of the few who lived up to the later romantic highwayman stereotype, apparently on one occasion used money he had stolen to pay off all the debts of the debtors in Salisbury gaol, and thus ensure their freedom.

Another early prototype of the gallant highwayman was William Nevison, born at Pontefract in Yorkshire in 1639 and executed at York in 1684. Despite a conventionally sound family background, Nevison took to stealing at the age of fourteen. After being punished for stealing a silver spoon from his father, he got up early one morning, stole ten pounds from his father and his schoolmaster's horse, and set off for London, cutting the throat of the horse and killing it just outside the capital in case he should be suspected of stealing it. He entered service with a brewer, with whom he worked for four years before robbing him and absconding to Holland. After various adventures, which included serving with the Duke of York, the future James II, against the English parliamentary and French forces that were

besieging Dunkirk, he returned to England and took up highway robbery. According to his later legend, he combined three
vital traits. He was very civil to his female victims, and enjoyed
the reputation among them of being a polite and obliging robber. He was charitable to the poor, and Robin Hood-like in giving them some of the spoils he collected from rich people he
robbed. And he was a convinced royalist, usually sparing those
he held up who had been active in the cause. It was no accident
that a nineteenth-century version of his life should dub him
'The Northern Claude Duval'.

And Nevison was also reputed, in an interesting reversal of
Dick Turpin's legendary journey, to have made an overnight
ride from the north to London to cash in a bill for £500, which
he had extracted from a former parliamentarian official who
had insufficient cash about him to meet Nevison's demands.
Nevison was anxious to have the bill paid before his victim
could get instructions down to London that it should be voided,
and apparently succeeded.

The gradual construction of the stereotype of the daring,
gallant and courteous highwayman led to a number of instances
of life imitating art. At least a few highwaymen, providing their
victims co-operated, seemed happy to indulge in pleasantries
with those they robbed, to treat them politely, and perhaps even
indulge in a little repartee with them. Thus, in 1763, it was
reported that an unidentified highwayman carrying out highway robberies in the London area assured his victims that he
was the heir to a large fortune, and that he would repay them
when he inherited. Another highwayman, robbing a clergyman, gave a little of the money he stole back to his victim
'to bear his charges', but refused when requested to return the

clergyman's watch, declaring that 'he was at present without one himself, and as he often wanted to know how time passed away, he could not oblige him with it'. On another occasion, a highwayman robbing a party of stagecoach passengers in 1751 informed them that he needed the money to go into mourning for the Prince of Wales, who had recently died.

But in the last resort the highwayman was a criminal, and one who could usually be callous, brutal and violent if circumstance dictated. The veneer of gentility, gallantry, and politeness, if it existed at all, was a thin one. To illustrate the point, let us return to a very famous highwayman, the 'gentleman highwayman', James MacLaine. While in Newgate shortly before his death, MacLaine (or so contemporary accounts assure us) shared a cell with a footpad named Ned Slinker. Apparently dismayed by being incarcerated with such a low-grade and low-class criminal, MacLaine wrote an apologia in which he contrasted the robberies carried out by highwaymen with the squalid little crimes carried out by footpads, contrasted his own status as a literate and polished man of taste and fashion with that of the lowborn Slinker, and claimed that he had forced the footpad to pay back the money he had taken from one of his more recent victims, a poor labourer. Gentlemen highwaymen, on the strength of this story, obviously saw themselves as, and perhaps were, a breed apart from the common thief. The ordinary of Newgate, one of a series of clergymen holding that office who ministered to the prison's inmates and wrote accounts of their lives, had a somewhat more jaundiced view of MacLaine's claims to gentility. 'Though he has been called the gentleman highwayman', the ordinary wrote, 'and in his dress and equipage very much affected the fine gentleman, yet to a man acquainted with good breeding, that can distinguish it from impudence and affectation, there was little in his address or behaviour, that could entitle him to that character.' As another contemporary was to put it, MacLaine was 'the gentleman in nothing more that the outward appearance', and perhaps the most telling comment on the period's attitudes to MacLaine's claim to gentility came when an army officer whom he chal- lenged to a duel declared himself unwilling to do so until the challenger could produce a certificate of his lineage.

As the eighteenth century progressed, the highwayman, at least in the big, expensive compendia of criminal biographies, began to lose his status as the overwhelmingly interesting crimi- nal. A quick analysis of the criminal lives described, for exam- ple, in *The Complete Newgate Calendar*, demonstrates the point. Highwaymen are still there, of course, but increasingly those other offenders who had always been present among the variety of criminals treated in these stories came to form a much higher proportion of those malefactors who were considered memo- rable. Hence, of fifty-one offenders whose misdeeds are recorded in *The Complete Newgate Calendar* for the years 1750–61, only four were highway robbers. The largest single category were murderers, but there was also a new type of offender who equalled the highwaymen in number. These were men who were convicted and executed for forgery: John Carr, who, after a career as a pirate and smuggler, was executed at Tyburn in 1750 for forging seamen's wills; William Baker, executed there the following year after he had forged an East India Company Warrant in an attempt to avoid bankruptcy; William Adams, a customs officer, executed at Tyburn for forgery in 1757; John Ayliffe, Esquire, son of 'a gentleman of large fortune' and

4. *The highwayman in popular culture: illustrations from* The Life of Richard Turpin, *a chapbook, in fact number 48 of the Royal Pocket Library, published at Leeds probably in the 1860s. This work cobbles together pirated extracts from Richard Bayes's* The Genuine History of the Life of Richard Turpin *of 1739 and William Harrison Ainsworth's* Rookwood *of 1834 (© Dean and Chapter of York: By kind permission).*

holder of a place at the War Office, executed for forgery in 1759. By the later eighteenth century forgery was becoming identified as the new crime of the age, replacing highway robbery. Capitalism had moved on, and become more sophisticated, and so the criminals who were really thought to threaten it were not the highwaymen who robbed wealthy farmers on their way back from market, but rather those men who corrupted the reliability of the written instruments upon which capitalism, and indeed the running of the state, increasingly depended.

Thus the lives and eventual ends of highwaymen no longer took centre stage when the genteel reading public was being regaled with tales of notorious criminals. Among the population at large, as the continued publication of chapbooks recording Hind's exploits suggests, the highwayman continued to exert a considerable fascination.

By the second half of the eighteenth century the authors of collections of stories about highwaymen clearly had an expanding number of figures to choose from. What is striking is that Dick Turpin was rarely among the pantheon of really important highwaymen. There is, for example, no mention of him in the 1797 *Anecdotes, Bon Mots, Traits, Strategems and Biographical Sketches*, although it has to be admitted that this book was almost perverse in its neglect of the big names that had loomed large in the pages of Alexander Smith and Charles Johnson. But Turpin had not figured in the 1742 edition of Johnson's *A General History*, and more surprisingly, perhaps, a short tract clearly aimed at a popular market, *The Lives of Noted Highwaymen*, published around 1750, contained no mention of Turpin. Duval was there, as were a number of other figures familiar in this type of literature: Thomas Rowland, Tom Jones, Edward Hinton, Jack Withrington. Turpin was absent. Doubtless he enjoyed considerable notoriety in the late 1730s, and his capture and execution in 1739 were commemorated in the popular press. But a half century after his death, Turpin was largely forgotten. It was the dashing exploits and merry pranks of a number of other highwaymen that were considered memorable enough to be continually reintroduced into the latest collection of highwayman stories.

Finally Daniel Defoe, that wonderful source for early eighteenth-century economic and social history, whose *A Tour through the whole Island of Great Britain*, was first published in the mid 1720s. Writing about Gadshill in Kent, Defoe noted that this was a place which was notorious for the robbery of seamen who had been paid off in nearby Chatham. He went on to tell of a famous robbery committed there in 1676 by 'one Nicks', a soubriquet that has been attributed to an ex-royalist officer turned highwayman named Richard Dudley, and, perhaps, to William Nevison, Yorkshire's own highwayman. Dudley (if we may identify him with 'Nicks') robbed a gentleman who apparently declared himself able to identify his assailant. The highwayman, clearly worried, took a boat across the Thames to Essex, and rode through that county, up through Cambridgeshire, turned west on to the Great North Road, and then, in Defoe's words

> keeping a full larger gallop most of the way, he came to York the same afternoon, put off his boots and riding clothes, and went dressed as if he had been an inhabitant of the place, not a traveller, to the bowling green, where, among the other gentlemen,

was the Lord Mayor of the city; he singling out his lordship, studied to do something particular that the mayor might remember him by, and accordingly lays some odd bets with him concerning the bowls then running, which should cause the mayor to remember it the more particularly; and then takes occasion to ask what a clock it was; who, pulling out his watch, told him the hour, which was a quarter after eight at night. Some other circumstances, it seems, he carefully brought into their discourse, which should make the lord mayor remember the day of the month exactly, as well the hour of the day.

A little later Dudley was prosecuted for the robbery at Gadshill, but he escaped conviction through putting up a convincing defence that, on the day in question, he was as far distant as Yorkshire, and that he could prove it by the evidence of the lord mayor of York, with whom he had played bowls. His defence held, although Dudley, thereafter known as 'Swift Nicks' on account of his ride, was eventually captured while attempting to rob the Duke of Lauderdale on Hounslow Heath, indicted on eighty counts of robbery at the Old Bailey, and executed at Tyburn on 22 February 1681.

Thus Turpin, the only eighteenth-century highwayman to survive in the modern popular historical consciousness, was virtually forgotten a half-century after his death, while the most famous exploit attributed to him, the ride to York, was apparently carried out by another, now long-forgotten highwayman (and there are, in fact, strong clues that Defoe's story of Nicks was preceded by even earlier tales of heroic rides to York). In the eighteenth century there were absolutely no indications that Turpin would achieve lasting fame, or that he would become the key figure in a resilient, long-lasting and adaptable legend. Those hanging him at York, while aware of his notoriety and his noteworthy criminal career, probably regarded Turpin, his career and his fate as typical of both criminality and of how that criminality was combated by the system of law and justice.

chapter *three*

CRIME

Eighteenth-century crime control has not enjoyed a good image among popular historians and their readers. More specifically, the central and symbolic element in eighteenth-century law enforcement, the public execution, has understandably been both written off itself as a barbaric phenomenon, and used as a symbol of the more general barbarity and dreadfulness of the period. The opinions of numerous reputable historians can be mobilised to illustrate this point. Thus for J. H. Plumb, one of the most influential historians of the eighteenth century of his generation, during that century 'violence, crime, cruelty, dirt, disease … were accepted by the majority of mankind as part of the nature of life, like the weather or the seasons', and it was therefore hardly surprising that the English should be a 'callous people', or that the popular sights of London included 'the lunatics of Bedlam, the whipping of half-naked people at the Bridewell, the stoning to death of pilloried men or women, or the hangings at Tyburn where a girl and a boy might be seen dangling between a highwayman and a murderer'. Another historian, V. H. H. Green, thought that there was in the eighteenth century 'a background of drink and violence, odorous sanitation, poor health and even more unpleasing vices', and followed the comments of an earlier historian, W. E. H. Lecky, in seeing the penal code of the period as 'mere sanguinary chaos'.

And thus the eighteenth-century public execution, and the 'sanguinary chaos' of the law-and-order system which at once produced it and was underpinned by it, became a powerful and much-used symbol of the dreadfulness of past ages: not only was sanitation almost non-existent, not only was gin swilled in vast amounts, but the criminal code of the period was brutal, chaotic and heavily dependent on that most repugnant of phenomena, the public execution. On this reading, the eighteenth century was simply a mess waiting to be cleared up by the onward march of the progress of the nineteenth and twentieth centuries. The current state of law and order in Britain suggests that progress in this area at least stopped moving onward some time ago: yet it is still all too easy to look back at the law-and-order system of the English *ancien régime*, and portray it as a mix of muddle and brutality against which a more civilised modernity might be contrasted, along with the better state of our sanitation and public health arrangements, and our assumed decline in gin drinking. But the old, pre-reform criminal justice system lasted for several centuries, and its demise did not go uncontested. This would suggest that it had its own rationale, and that if we are to understand how Dick Turpin began his criminal career, rose to fame as a highwayman, and eventually met his death on that chilly April Saturday in 1739, we need to slough off our comforting modern assumptions about the past, and try to understand the eighteenth-century criminal justice system by the standards of its own logic.

William Hogarth's print of Tom Idle's execution at the London Tyburn was first produced in 1747, eight years after Turpin's death. The foreground of Hogarth's execution scene is cluttered with figures, most of them portrayed side on, or with their backs to the viewer: there is a cripple with a crutch, a one-legged man straining to get a sight of what is happening in front of him, a stocky man apparently swinging a dog by its tail, a man and a woman fighting while a child sprawls on the ground near them, a group of mounted and uniformed sheriff's officers to the left of the picture, and man selling apples from a wheel-barrow, which is being overturned by children, to its right. In the middle distance, behind yet more figures, is the object of the crowd's attention: Tyburn's famous gallows, the wooden triangle raised horizontally on three upright beams, with a noose already being attached for Tom Idle's benefit. Idle himself is on a cart to the centre left of the print, a clergyman exhorting him as he is being driven to execution, his coffin ready for use behind him at the front of the cart. To the left, in the distance, a number of spectators sit on a high wall, while to the right a grand-stand has been constructed that is filled with spectators, presumably the better off who were willing to spend a little money to get a better view. Only one of the figures in the foreground of the print faces the viewer squarely: a woman ballad-seller, a child cradled in her arm, bawling the newly composed ditty on the life and execution of yet another notorious criminal. And beneath the print there is a suitable if chilling biblical text, Proverbs 1, 27–28: 'When fear cometh as desolation, and destruction cometh as a whirlwind: when distress cometh upon them, then they shall call upon God, but he will not answer.'

Hogarth's powerful image is matched by the published descriptions of public execution. Perhaps the most powerful of these, creating a vivid impression of dismaying brutality and anarchic uproar at Tyburn executions, comes from Bernard de Mandeville's *An Enquiry into the Causes of the Frequent Executions at Tyburn*. Mandeville was a Dutchman, born about 1670, who qualified as a medical doctor at the University of Leiden, and who subsequently settled in England, where he was to die in 1733. His attempts to set up as a doctor in London did not flourish, and he turned to polemical writing, his best-known work being his *Fable of the Bees, or Private Vices Public Benefits*. His *Enquiry* first appeared as a series of the letters in the *British Journal*, starting on 27 February 1725. This was a mere twelve days before the arrest of the notorious 'Thief-Taker General', Jonathan Wild, of whom more later, and the interest aroused by Wild's subsequent trial and execution rendered Mandeville's writings on Tyburn unusually timely. Mandeville begins his description of Tyburn executions thus:

> When the day of execution is come, among extraordinary sinners, and persons condemned for their crimes, who have but that morning to live, one would expect a deep sense of sorrow, with all the signs of a thorough contrition, and the utmost concern; that either silence, or a sober sadness, should prevail; and that all, who had any business there, should be grave, and serious, and behave themselves, at least, with common decency, and a deportment suitable to the occasion. But the very reverse is true. The horrid aspect of the turnkeys and gaolers, in discontent and hurry; the

sharp and dreadful looks of rogues, that beg in irons, but would
rob you with greater satisfaction, if they could; the bellowings
of half a dozen names at a time, that are perpetually made in the
enquiries after one another; the variety of strong voices, that are
heard, of howling in one place, scolding and quarrelling in
another, and loud laughter in a third; the substantial breakfasts
that are made in the midst of all this; the seas of beer that are
swill'd; the never-ceasing outcries for more; and the bawling
answers of the tapsters as continual; the quantity and varieties of
more entoxicating liquors, that are swallow'd in every part of
Newgate; the impudence, and unseasonable jests of those, who
administer them.

Mandeville continues in this vein, and then informs his reader
'but what is most shocking to a thinking man, is, the behaviour
of the condemn'd, whom (for the greatest part) you'll find,
either drinking madly, or uttering the vilest ribaldry, and jeering
others, that are less impenitent'.

The doors of Newgate are eventually opened, and the carts
carrying the condemned are processed through the streets,
attended by what Mandeville described as a 'torrent of mob':

Amongst the lower rank, and working people, the idlest, and
such as are fond of making holidays, with prentices and jour-
neymen to the meanest trades, are the most honorable part of
these floating multitudes. All the rest are worst. The days being
known beforehand, they are a summons to all thieves and pickpockets, of both sexes, to meet ... all the way, from Newgate to
Tyburn, is one continued fair, for whores and rogues of the
meaner sort. Here the most abandon'd rakehells may light on

women as shameless: here trollops, all in rags, may pick up sweethearts of the same politeness: and there are none so lewd, so vile, or so indigent, of either sex, but at the time and place aforesaid, they may find a paramour.

Mandeville carries on with a description of the crowds watching the felons as they pass, noting in particular their taste for 'their darling cordial, the grand preservative of sloth, Jeneva, that infallible antidote against care and frugal reflexion'. Gin-sellers, 'commonly the worst of both sexes', vend their commodity to the crowd, who consume it eagerly. Thus fortified, 'these undisciplined armies', which 'have no particular enemies to encounter, but cleanliness and good manners', entertain themselves by taking up 'the dead carcasses of dogs and cats, or, for want of them, rags, and all trompery that is capable of imbibing dirt'. These are 'by the ringleaders, flung as high and as far as a strong arm can carry them, and commonly directed where the throng is the thickest'.

The prisoners themselves, on Mandeville's account, usually took care to be as drunk as possible before leaving Newgate, but, on their way to the gallows, 'the courage that strong liquors can give, wears off', and the condemned find themselves in danger of becoming sober again:

For this reason they must drink as they go; and the cart stops for that purpose three or four, and sometimes half a dozen times, or more, before they come to their journey's end. These halts always encrease the numbers about the criminals ... their quondam companions, more eager than others, break through all obstacles to take leave: and here you may see young villains, that are proud of being so (if they knew any of the malefactors) tear the cloaths off their backs, by squeezing and creeping thro' the legs of men and horses, to shake hands with him; and not to lose, before so much company, the reputation there is in having had such a valuable acquaintance.

The problems created by the crowd pressing in on the condemned intensify near the gallows, and the 'rugged gaolers' have more or less to cudgel their way through the mob to get the condemned to the place of execution. For Mandeville, 'the mean equippage of the sheriff's officers, and the scrubby horses that compose the cavalcade, the irregularity of the march, and the want of order among the attendants' created an overall impression 'that these processions are very void of that decent solemnity that would be required to make them awful'. Things get no better at the place of execution. There is assembled 'a vast multitude on foot, intermixed with many horsemen and hackney-coaches, all very dirty, or else cover'd with dust'. The condemned criminals continued to behave with little seeming attention to their impending deaths, many of them, in fact, being buoyed up by usually misplaced confidence in a last-minute pardon or reprieve. Overall, the scene at Tyburn, Mandeville concluded, was such that 'the best dispos'd spectator seldom can pick out anything that is edifying or moving'.

Mandeville, like all commentators of the period, was arguing a case, while his writings, here as elsewhere, generally suggest that he may not have had too broad a sympathy with his fellow human beings. Certainly, recent research has suggested that executions at Tyburn, and the phenomenon of the early modern public execution more generally, were somewhat more complex, and certainly less brutal, occasions than such descriptions as Mandeville's might lead us to believe. Most of our descriptions of public executions come from London, and especially Tyburn. Executions at Tyburn loom large in the accounts of such visitors to London from the provinces and foreign tourists who left a record of their impressions of metropolitan life, while it was with the Tyburn executions that polemicists such as Mandeville were concerned. Insofar as we have descriptions of executions outside London, they appear, like Turpin's, to have been more orderly affairs, less prone to displays of mob brutality.

Yet there were a number of recurring elements. It was common, as happened with Turpin, for notorious offenders to become objects of public spectacle while awaiting execution. The gaoler at York was reputed to have made £100 from selling drink to Turpin and those who came to see him. He may also have charged a fee to those wishing to view or visit this notorious criminal. Certainly this was the practice at Newgate, and it has been calculated that the gaolers made several hundred pounds when the near-legendary Jack Sheppard was imprisoned before his execution in 1724, while they presumably made a considerable amount from the three thousand people who came to see the highwayman James MacLaine as he awaited execution in 1750. It was common, as Turpin did, to buy new clothes to be hanged in: 'He that is to be hanged, or otherwise executed', wrote a foreign observer in 1698, 'first takes care to get himself shav'd, and handsomely drest, either in mourning or in the dress of a bridegroom', while women going to be executed often dressed in white, wore long scarves, and carried baskets of fruit or flowers, which they distributed to the crowds. The condemned, again like Turpin at York, were processed from gaol to the place of execution in a cart, frequently, like Hogarth's Tom Idle, accompanied by a clergyman and their coffin.

All sources agree that in eighteenth-century London execution days were a great event, attended by people of all social ranks, with as many as 30,000 spectators being recorded at one execution. For these spectators, the most crucial element in the theatre of punishment that they had gathered to witness was the conduct of the condemned on the scaffold. Expectations of this conduct were varied, and attuned to the offender in question. Those who were considered to be daring offenders, like highwaymen, were expected to 'die game', to show courage before the cart was driven off from under them or, as in Turpin's case at York, before they were turned off the ladder. Others, especially women, were expected to die contritely and penitently. A major part of the offender's role centred around the 'last dying speech' he or she was expected to make, which frequently formed the basis of ballads or pamphlets that were rushed into print. These speeches (whose stereotypical nature raises a slight nervousness about the authenticity of the descriptions we have of them) normally presented a narrative in which youthful sins led, inexorably, to the ever-escalating wrongdoing that eventually brought the offender to the gallows.

Such speeches could be edifying, but what happened at Tyburn frequently was not. A crucial point was the technology of execution. The drop, the method of hanging first introduced in 1783, and used in Britain until the 1960s, causes, when carried out by a trained executioner, instantaneous death. Hanging by strangulation, as performed over much of the eighteenth century, was a slower means of killing. It was expected that those being hanged would normally take half an hour to die, their legs kicking in the air, their eyes goggling, their mouths foaming, control of their bowels and bladder going in the last few minutes of life. Friends and relatives of the hanged might pull on their legs to end the suffering, while a foreign observer records them beating stones on their breasts to accelerate death. The uncertainty of the method of killing was worsened by an occasional tendency for ropes to break, or for the hangman's knot to come undone. And there was the phenomenon known as 'half-hanging', when an offender was cut down as dead, only to revive later. Thus the body of man called Reynolds, executed in 1736, was cut down from the gallows, 'but as the coffin was fastening, he thrust back the lid, upon which the executioner would have tied him up again, but the mob prevented it, and carried him to a house where he vomited three pints of blood, but on giving him a glass of wine, he died'. Some even regained consciousness when they were in the hands of the surgeons awaiting dissection before an anatomy class: one such, with the surgeon's connivance, escaped to America and subsequently made his fortune.

The main justification for the public execution was that, in an age when it was generally accepted that the main object of punishing criminals was deterrence, executing criminals in public was an obvious method of achieving the maximum deterrent effect by ensuring that the maximum number of people witnessed the criminal's fate. There was also a feeling that the public execution exposed the offender to the fullest possible moral disapprobation of the community. Thus the enormity of his or her crime would be emphasised, not only to the offender but to the public at large. Accordingly, the public execution became a vehicle not only for deterrence and the display of state power, but also for the propagandising of a shared moral vision. The problem with this, of course, is that what was intended to be a display of state power and a lesson in deterrence ran the risk of being appropriated by the crowd. Normally, upper-class observers did not like the Tyburn mob, and described their behaviour in the same sort of tones as did Mandeville: the genteel in Hanoverian England lost no opportunity for distancing themselves from the rude multitude. But more sympathetic analyses have demonstrated that the mob had a sense of morality, a sense of how things ought to be done, and showed their disapprobation loudly and sometimes violently if things went wrong. They felt that the 'half-hanged' should be left to go free. They rioted against the practice of giving corpses to the surgeons for their anatomy classes, something that happened at York after Turpin's execution. They disliked incompetent hangmen, hurling stones, bricks and tiles at executioners who were felt to be bungling their job. And they showed a range of emotions to those standing on the gallows, varying from hostility to those whom they felt to be unusually heinous offenders, to sympathy, even tears, for those whom they thought to be suffering too harsh a punishment, or who behaved themselves with unusual penitence at the gallows.

Most of our images of public executions come from the eighteenth century: Hogarth's print of Tom Idle at Tyburn, the climactic Tyburn execution scene in Fielding's *Tom Jones*, the way

5. Our most striking image of an eighteenth-century public execution, William Hogarth's portrayal of the execution of Tom Idle at Tyburn in London, from his 'Industry and Idleness' series of 1747 (University of York Library).

6. Another print from Hogarth's 'Industry and Idleness' series, showing a criminal (Tom Idle) being charged before a city magistrate, in this case his erstwhile fellow apprentice. The committal of those members of the Essex gang apprehended in London in 1735 would have looked very much like this (University of York Library).

the gallows lurks continually in Defoe's *Moll Flanders*, the vivid impression of the procession to Tyburn given in Jonathan Swift's *Clever Tom Clinch, Going to be Hanged*. To these images might be added the legislative process that created what became known as the 'Bloody Code', a process which meant that by 1800 there were over 200 offences on the English statute book, most of them crimes against property, which could be punished by death. Yet one of the major surprises when historians began the slow and laborious task of unpicking the court records was that the early eighteenth century, the era when Turpin died and from which so many of our images of public execution come, was in fact experiencing levels of execution much lower than those in the late sixteenth and early seventeenth century. The impact of executions in these earlier times can be best conveyed if we continue a statistical exercise initiated by the Victorian editor and antiquary, J. C. Jeaffreson. By a simple process of extrapolation Jeaffreson calculated that if the levels of execution obtaining in the first two decades of the seventeenth century had still been in operation in the metropolitan area of the late Victorian era, with its population of four million, there would have been 2,263 executions annually. If we may continue this process of extrapolation, set against London's early twenty-first-century population of some seven million, the figure approaches 4,000 a year: one suspects that this level of executions would give even the most avid proponent of capital punishment cause for reflection.

But by the early eighteenth century, the most severe period of the death penalty was long past. In the 1590s people standing trial for felony stood a one in four or five chance of being executed: by the 1730s this had dropped to one in eight or ten, and the courts had well-established forms of secondary punishments that provided alternatives to execution. By the time of Turpin's execution, on the evidence of most surviving documentation, the punishment most likely to be inflicted on people guilty of felony at England's assizes was a relatively new one, transportation to the American colonies. The ending of the War of the Spanish Succession in 1713 set the trend for other eighteenth-century post-war situations by being followed by a crime wave: peace meant the mass demobilisation of thousands of soldiers and sailors, most of them young men from the labouring classes, exactly the group from which most of those accused of felony were drawn. This had ramifications other than creating a climate where Alexander Smith's *History of the Lives* might find a ready readership. Most seriously, a system that was already searching for forms of secondary punishment found itself in danger of being overwhelmed by executions. Disquiet at this problem resulted in the Transportation Act of 1718 (4 Geo I, cap. 11). This law, directed primarily against property offenders, enacted that persons convicted for non-capital felonies could be sent to the American colonies (in practice mainly Virginia and Maryland) for seven years, while those convicted for capital felonies might be transported for fourteen years – in either case, return to England before this term had been served was punishable by death. The policy proved highly successful, with some 30,000 English and 6,000 Irish convicted felons being sent to start a new life in America before the outbreak of the American War of Independence put an end to the practice. The policy also, in a reminder of how central government was extending its interest into crime control in this period, represented what was, by the standard of the time, a massive government investment in the punishment of criminals: those shipping the convicts had to be paid.

Transportation, together with longer-established secondary punishments, meant that by the 1730s, the decade of Turpin's criminal career, the English assize courts enjoyed a number of alternatives to executing convicted felons, and were happy to use them in what was a very flexible punishment system. At the core of this flexibility lay a the notion of selectivity: in theory a large number of those convicted could have been subjected to capital punishment, but in practice only a selected minority were hanged. Convicted felons who were young, had no previous criminal record, came from a respectable family background, were tried for a not particularly heinous offence in a period of relative social tranquillity, and for whom influential people could be found to provide a character reference, were likely to escape execution. Hardened offenders who were convicted for what were perceived as notorious offences at a time when the authorities were jumpy and wished to make examples were likely to end on the gallows. Being tried for felony before an assize had something of the flavour of participating in a lottery: later in the century, a capitally convicted felon was reported as saying 'there are so many chances for us, and so few against us, that I never thought of coming to this'.

A crucial factor in a convicted felon's ability to escape hanging was the possibility of obtaining suitable character witnesses. This renders some of Turpin's comments at his trial fully comprehensible. 'I have none present', said Turpin of his character witnesses, 'but tomorrow I will have them, I am sure no man can say ill of me in Yorkshire.' Or, as he said at another point, 'I thought I should have been removed to Essex ... therefore I could not prepare witnesses to my character.' Turpin's appreciation of the main way in which a man or woman in his position might have escaped the noose is correct, although it is very doubtful if anything could have saved him. But more generally evidence about previous good character from the accused's neighbours or from previous employers and other persons of influence could be crucial in gaining an acquittal, or in ensuring that a convicted felon would suffer a secondary punishment rather than be hanged.

As the centrality of public execution suggests, one of the main objectives of the criminal law was to preserve social order and the existing social hierarchy through terror. But, through the processes of selectivity, that terror was tempered by mercy. Even in the early eighteenth century, what might be described as public opinion would have been horrified if a score or more of executions for property offences had followed every provincial assize and session at Bow Street. Moreover, the regular deploy-ment of mercy reinforced the public perception that criminal justice in England was fair, an important ideological consid-eration when most Englishmen conceived that they lived in a country that was subject to the rule of law.

The criminal justice system in the eighteenth century, the criminal justice system that hanged Dick Turpin, therefore operated on a rationale very different from that of a modern state, with its professional police forces, social services and a fully bureaucratised law-enforcement system. In the early eigh-teenth century at least, the enforcement of law and order depended largely on unpaid amateur officials, the justices of the peace and the parish constables and other local officers. This system was done away with a century later, when professional police forces came in after the setting up of Peel's Metropolitan Police in 1829, and the penitentiary prison was brought in to replace the public execution as the standard method of dealing with those convicted of serious crime. And, since history tends to be written by the winners, the old system of law enforcement, based on amateur local officials, and underpinned by the public execution, has been written off as barbaric or chaotic. But this allegedly barbaric system had its own logic, and it tends to be forgotten (or written out of the popular histories) that it had intelligent and eloquent defenders when notions of reform arose in the later eighteenth century. It also worked tolerably well, certainly in the 1730s, when Turpin flourished, certainly better than modern opinion has given it credit for: except, that is, in London.

When arguing that London in this period experienced unique law-and-order problems we must remember that our impressions may be distorted: London was so much better documented than other areas, and most commentators seeking to inform, or indeed form, opinion about law-and-order issues were London-based, while our most vivid images of eighteenth-century crime and punishment normally concern London, and, above all, the triple tree at Tyburn. Certainly London, or perhaps more accurately the metropolitan area, was, in Turpin's time, a major phenomenon. It was the largest city in Europe, with a population rising from perhaps 575,000 in 1700 to 675,000 in 1750. This also made London by far the biggest city in England: the second-largest, Norwich, had a population of something like 30,000 in the early eighteenth century. Maybe ten per cent of England's population at any one time lived in London, while high mortality among the capital's population meant that for that population to remain stable, let alone increase, there had to be a steady influx of immigrants from the English countryside. And by the early eighteenth century incomers from other parts of England were supplemented by an established community of French Huguenot refugees, many of them living in Spitalfields, a small Jewish and a growing Irish population, and a black presence. The capital demonstrated massive disparities of wealth among its inhabitants. Since 1660 England had enjoyed a boom in trade, a commercial revolution that had established it as the strongest economic power in Europe, dominating the North Atlantic economy and sending its ships to trade to Africa and Asia. Most of the vessels bringing the fruits of this trade home to England came to London, unloading in the capital's ever-expanding docks. Accordingly, the city's merchants grew rich, and the middling sort involved in a myriad of trades, industries and services grew prosperous. Others – the casual workers, the men and women in the unskilled trades, the recent immigrants seeking any available work in the capital – did less well.

Despite its immensity by the standards of the time, eighteenth-century London still covered a much smaller area than it does at present. At its heart lay the old City of London, enjoying a fierce sense of its traditions and an independent administration in criminal justice as in much else. The City of Westminster also existed as a separate entity. The area surrounding these two cities lay in the county of Middlesex, those parts adjacent to London and Westminster being already built up. These built-up areas spread in a straggling line towards what was to become the East End, with places like Hackney finding themselves the next candidates for urbanisation. London Bridge connected the city to the Borough of Southwark, and by the mid eighteenth century there was another straggling built-up area south of the Thames running down to Rotherhithe. It was these outlying areas, especially urban Middlesex, which were experiencing the greatest population growth, an especially serious matter as the parishes being newly urbanised had less effective policing and poor-law systems than the parishes in the City of London proper. In the City parishes, and perhaps in some parishes in other parts of the metropolitan area, a strong sense of community, and something like the 'face to face' ethos of rural communities persisted: but there was a growing feeling among early eighteenth-century observers that the capital was a relatively anonymous place, and that this anonymity was of advantage to criminals.

This attitude was summed up neatly by somebody whose opinions on such matters are worth paying attention to, the novelist and London magistrate Henry Fielding:

> Whoever indeed considers the cities of London and Westminster with the late vast addition of their suburbs, the great irregularity of their buildings, the immense number of lanes, alleys, courts and bye-places; must think that, had they been intended for the very purpose of concealment, they could scarce have been better contrived. Upon such a view, the whole appears as a vast wood or forest, in which a thief may harbour with as great security, as wild beasts do in the deserts of Africa or Arabia.

Fielding was undoubtedly a well-informed observer, but he was also a man with an axe to grind, a man who was arguing for law-and-order reforms. Yet many contemporaries regarded the metropolitan area as offering unique law-and-order problems, and their views were well founded. A system of crime control that was based on the social structures of rural and small town society, on the paternalistic input of justices of the peace and the local gentry, and on the face-to-face community, was ill adjusted to meet the needs of an urban area with a population of half a million, a population that was, in some parts, transient and rootless. London was to experience constant experiments in new forms of policing and crime control in the late seventeenth and early eighteenth centuries, and a number of national policies owed their origins to perceptions of the crime problem in the capital.

It is possible, through patient research, to reconstruct the statistical contours of crime in and around the capital, but qualitative materials convey a more immediate sense of the impact of crime. The problems of crime and law and order in the metropolitan area are illustrated by the work of Henry Norris, a justice of the peace operating on what were then the fringes of the metropolis. Norris lived in Hackney, a parish that, despite the encroachments of urbanisation, sat in open countryside, was seen as a suitable pleasure resort by Londoners and was the location of a number of private schools and of gentleman's houses, but which enjoyed an active economy characterised by agricultural and horticultural production geared for the needs of the London market, and some industrial production, notably brick-making. Norris, whose family had settled in Hackney two generations earlier, was an active justice who kept a detailed notebook of his activities which reveal that even this apparently tranquil and prosperous area suffered from its fair share of crime. The criminal accusations heard by Norris have been analysed for the period February 1730 to July 1741, a period that spanned Turpin's criminal career (indeed, one of Turpin's associates whom we shall be meeting in the next chapter figures in Norris's notebook). This analysis shows Norris dealing with 207 offences against the peace, among them 186 assaults, and seventy-five cases of theft or property disputes, and fifteen cases that might be categorised as vice, six of them involving cursing and swearing, and four drunkenness. Over a third of these cases were agreed between the parties involved under the justice's mediation without any further legal action, and just under a fifth were dealt with by summary conviction.

Norris's notebook reveals a mixture of serious and petty crime. Thus in December 1732 the local headborough (constable) brought before him William Heath, who was accused by Martha Plummer of threatening her with a knife, knocking her to the ground, and stealing a small sum of money and a bundle of children's bed linen from her. Her cries for help were heard ('she cryed out murder'), and four men gave evidence how they chased and caught the prisoner. Heath appeared at the December Old Bailey Sessions, and was sentenced to death. The numerous assaults Norris dealt with contained a number of instances of domestic violence, a subject that rarely figures in the more formal criminal records of the period. On 8 February 1731, for example, Norris noted hearing and acting upon the complaint of Thomasin Wheeler, who informed against her husband John Wheeler 'for beating & abusing her being sick & for denying to assist in the maintenance of her & her children & threatning her saying were no more pity to kill her then to kill a

dog'. But there was also a whole range of petty criminals committing petty crimes, like Susan Newcome, a vagrant woman
sent to the House of Correction in 1736 after she had been
caught stealing apples from a local gentleman's garden, or John
Whittell, complained against in the same year by Katherine
Carter for 'unlawfuly digging up & carrying away her turneps
out of her field back of Bethnall Green'.

Offenders like Newcome or Whittell were more typical of
the criminals of their period than the notorious felons who
entered popular legend. The fear was that petty criminals might
grow into, or at least by their example provide encouragement
for, serious ones. The regular executions at Tyburn demonstrated that a constant stream of men and women were graduat-
ing from petty to serious crime, and paying the price for this
graduation to a higher level of delinquency. An analysis has
been made of the 1,242 men and women hanged at Tyburn on
243 hanging days between 1703 and 1772. Of these, well over a
third came from London, just over a third from the remainder of
England, just over one in eight from Ireland, and the rest from
other parts of the British Isles and beyond. Of those of the male
hanged who were English-born but who came from outside
London, just over a quarter were apprentices, a third were time-
served tradesmen, about one in eight were soldiers or sailors,
with rural labourers forming about the same proportion. The
tradesmen, London-born as well as those of provincial origins,
were involved in a wide variety of occupations: weavers, butch-
ers, shoemakers, carpenters. The London hanged were a more
geographically mobile group than the capital's population as a
whole, with soldiers, sailors and a high proportion of Irish
among them. But, as the large numbers of apprentices and

tradesmen executed demonstrated, even those in a trade might go to the bad, turn to crime, and make their end before the eager spectators at Tyburn.

London was replete with criminals, and this was a source of concern to the authorities and citizens alike. But what was perhaps unique to London in this period was the conviction that criminals were not acting simply as isolated deviants, but rather that they were organised into gangs. Since the Elizabethan period at least organised crime had existed in London, with well-planned property offences, the organised receiving of stolen goods, and organised prostitution that sometimes involved networks of prostitutes and brothel owners. London had long offered opportunities to organised crime and the professional criminal, but the urban and commercial expansion of the early eighteenth century, and the increase in the number and variety of consumer goods available to steal, meant that such opportunities were multiplying rapidly. The crime wave that accompanied the ending of the War of the Spanish Succession was to witness the rise of England's first great criminal entrepreneur, and the world's prototype gangster, Jonathan Wild.

Wild, born the son of a joiner in Wolverhampton in 1683, began his criminal career as a prostitute's bully, robbing the clients of Mary Milline, a prostitute with whom he had set up house, extorting money from them by threats, or helping dispose of the goods she herself had stolen from them. He gradually rose up the criminal pecking order, so that by the early 1720s, if contemporary opinion is to believed, Wild had crime in the metropolitan area under his control to an extent that even the Kray brothers would have envied. The nature of his activities, not least as they were perceived by his contemporaries, was summed up in the 'Warrant of Detainer' that the City Recorder, Sir William Thomson, laid before the court prior to Wild's trial in 1725. He had been a confederate with a great number of highwaymen, pickpockets, housebreakers, shop-lifters, and other thieves. He had 'form'd a kind of corporation of thieves, of which he was the head or director', and while pretending to detect and prosecute offenders, in fact 'procured only such to be hang'd as concealed their booty, or refused to share it with him'. He also allegedly divided London and its environs into 'so many districts', and allocated 'distinct gangs to each, whoe regularly accounted with him for their robberies', and that he had 'a particular sett to steal at churches in time of divine service: and likewise other moving detachments to attend at court, on birth-days, balls, etc, and at both Houses of Parliament, Circuits, and country fairs'. Most of those he employed, the warrant continued, were convicted felons who had returned from transportation before their time. Wild apparently chose such people deliberately as his agents, 'because they could not get legal evidence against him, and because he had it in his power to take from them what part of the stolen goods he thought fit, and otherwise use them ill, or hang them as he pleas'd'. He had, moreover, from time to time supplied such people with money and clothes, and lodged them in his own house to conceal them more effectively.

The warrant continued that he had not only been a receiver of stolen goods, as well as of 'writings of all kinds', for fifteen years, but that he had 'frequently been a confederate, and robb'd along with the above mention'd convicted felons'. He also, in a striking indication of the magnitude of his supposed criminal activities, was thought to have 'under his care, and direction, several warehouses for receiving and concealing stolen goods', as well as 'a ship for carrying off jewels, watches, and other valuable goods, to Holland', where he had a retired thief for his factor. He kept in his pay several 'artists' whose task it was 'to make alterations, and transform watches, seals, snuff-boxes, rings, and other valuable things, that they might not be known, several of which he used to present to such persons as he thought might be of service to him'. The earlier references to 'writings of all kinds' was fleshed out by another of the clauses in the warrant, which alleged that Wild 'seldom or never helped the owners to the notes and papers they had lost, unless he found them able exactly to specify and describe them, and then often insisted on more than half the value'. 'And lastly', the warrant concluded, 'it appears that he has often sold human blood, by procuring false evidences to swear persons into facts [i.e. crimes] they were not guilty of; sometimes to prevent them from being evidences against himself, and at other times for the sake of the great reward given by the government.' Overall Wild was an unparalleled criminal mastermind.

His luck ran out, of course, and in May 1725 he was executed after accomplices in a robbery he planned gave evidence against him. Wild's thief-taking activities were hardly likely to have made him many friends, and the mob seems to have been united in its joy when he was executed. The *London Journal* informed its readers that

> never was there a greater crowd assembled on any occasion, than
> to see this unhappy person; and so outrageous were the mob in
> their joy to behold him on the road to the gallows, who had been
> the cause of sending so many thither; that they huzza'd him

along to the Triple Tree, and shew'd a temper very uncommon
on such melancholy occasion, for they threw stones at him; with
some of which his head was broke, and the two malefactors,
Sperry and Sandford, between whom he sate in the cart, were
hurt; nay, even in his last lament they did not cease their insults …

After execution, Wild's body was buried in St Pancras churchyard, but, just to round off the story in true eighteenth-century
style, the grave was robbed of its body, with the intention, so it
was supposed, that Wild's corpse should be used in the anatomy
theatre. Indeed, in 1847 a skeleton reputed to be Wild's was presented by a Dr Fowler to the Royal College of Surgeons, Fowler
claiming that the skeleton had been in his and his predecessor's
possession for more than fifty years.

The history of Wild's criminal empire, like the history of
crime in London in general in his period, demonstrates the
importance of a new factor in criminal prosecution, the heavy
dependence on rewards, a dependence that was of obvious significance to the practice of thief-taking. This was an important
governmental innovation in crime control that involved a heavy
financial outlay. Legislation between 1692 and 1706 had provided for the regular granting of rewards of £40 to those giving
information leading to the conviction of robbers, burglars and
coiners: this sum, to put the policy in perspective, was roughly
the equivalent of two years' wages for a skilled manual worker.
Then in 1720 there came a proclamation that offered a reward of
£100 over and above the statutory £40 for information leading
to the conviction of persons committing robberies within a five-
mile radius of Charing Cross. This meant that it was possible
to obtain a reward of £140 for the conviction of a highway rob-

ber. In practice, the courts normally divided such rewards among a number of persons giving evidence. Thus in Middlesex, in the three years beginning December 1730, there were 449 payments of rewards to 320 individuals arising from fifty-six criminal cases. Often the reward for an individual conviction would be shared between six and ten people, which meant that in this sample about a third of individuals received less than £5 for their information, and another third between £5 and £10. Nevertheless, £5 was a useful sum in the early eighteenth century, and the average payment of £12 or so was not much less than a labourer's annual earnings.

Perhaps the most remarkable aspect of this system of rewards was that central government was willing to pay them, just as government was willing to invest heavily in setting up the system of transportation to the American colonies. Funding frequent and generous rewards amounted to a substantial investment in the criminal justice system, and, as with the financing of transportation, is indicative of a growing and novel involvement of the government in what had hitherto been an essentially personal matter, the prosecution of individual criminals. The government in George I's reign in many ways conceived of itself as being under siege, an attitude massively reinforced by the Jacobite rebellion of 1715 and by the disturbances that gave rise to that most celebrated piece of legislation, the Riot Act of the same year. Continued concern over Jacobite plots and more general sedition kept these anxieties alive, and hence government attentions began by being focussed on the prosecutions over matters of state. After 1715, or thereabouts, the government became increasingly interested in the prosecution of more run-of-the-mill crime. The perception of what constituted a threat to the state had now widened beyond sedition and riot to included the perpetrators of felony: thus, we may remind ourselves, a politician as important as the Duke of Newcastle could take an interest in a serious but in no way extraordinary criminal like Dick Turpin. It was now a matter of prestige to high-ranking government officials that serious offenders should be caught, not least because the political opposition might find targets for criticism in government's inability to make England safe from criminals.

There was much to worry politicians and those they claimed to protect in the law-and-order situation over the first half of the eighteenth century, in particular in the metropolis, where there was a high level of sophistication in criminal organisation. One of the recurrent themes that Wild's career threw up, and obviously one that was of great interest to contemporaries, was the presence of gangs. The gang-breaking activities that accompanied Wild's push towards achieving hegemony over the metropolitan underworld in the early 1720s, for example, included the fall of the Spiggott and Hawkins gangs of highwaymen, and Shaw's and Carrick's gangs of footpads, the latter containing a fair proportion of Irish immigrants. Such gangs, despite contemporary imaginings, were normally fairly small, and like, one suspects, criminal gangs in all periods, were fairly loose associations, with members splitting off and forming subgroups, with peripheral contacts being called in as occasion demanded. The core of permanent gang members would normally not be large. But in the early eighteenth century, contemporary fears of organised crime already awarded a central importance to the notion of the criminal gang. And, in the mid 1730s, the forces of law and order in and around the capital and metropolitan newspaper readers were becoming all too aware of the activities of an especially troublesome criminal gang that was operating on the eastern fringes of the London area.

chapter *four*

THE ESSEX GANG *and its* AFTERMATH

It started with deer-stealing. Or, to be more precise, with the stealing of King George II's deer from the Royal Forest of Waltham in Essex. Deer-stealing in the Forest had long been endemic, but by the early 1730s the verderers (local forest officials) were unusually worried about gangs of deer-thieves operating in the area. In a sworn affidavit of 5 March 1731 seven of the verderers declared that they

> make oath that diverse disorderly and idle persons have of late frequently both in the day time as well as in the night killed wounded and carried off several of his Majesty's red and fallow deer within the said Forest of Waltham in defiance of us the Keepers thereof and do still persist in committing great abuses and frequently go in numbers together with fire arms and other dangerous weapons insomuch that the Keepers of the said Forest go in danger of their lives.

This expression of disquiet was directed at someone important – Thomas Pelham-Holles, the Duke of Newcastle, Secretary of

State for the Southern Department. About a month later Newcastle signed a proclamation that offered a reward of £10 to anyone who gave information leading to the conviction of a deerstealer, and, as was usual in such proclamations, offered a pardon to any deerstealers who turned king's evidence against their colleagues.

The proclamation did not stop depredations on the deer in Waltham Forest, and during the two years following 1731 there was a stream of prosecutions for offences committed there. Some of these were fairly minor, others not, although it must surely strike the modern reader, living in a society worried by gun crime, that most of them involved the possession or use of firearms. Thus in November 1732 John Wooton, one of the Keepers who had signed the affidavit sent to Newcastle the previous year, confiscated a gun from 'Jeremiah' (he was more usually referred to as Jeremy) Gregory, a man unqualified to own a gun in the Forest. This same 'Jeremiah' Gregory, the day after Wooton brought in the confiscated gun, was allegedly involved in a shooting incident in which he, Joseph Rose and John Coster, or one of them, fired a gun at a man called Deakins, who subsequently died (Gregory was acquitted). Another man, an innocent passerby, died after being hit accidentally during a shooting incident in Wanstead some three weeks later. And in June 1733 a major raid was carried out by the Waltham Forest deerstealers, on another royal forest, Enfield Chase, just over the county border from Essex in Middlesex. In the course of this raid the gang declared their intention of shooting one of the Keepers, William Wood. Fortunately, Wood was absent, so the gang attacked the house of another Keeper, Turpin Mason, saying that they intended to murder him and his family. The

Masons fled, although the gang attempted to shoot Turpin Mason's seventeen-year-old son as he escaped on horseback. Failing in this, they contented themselves with shooting the Keeper's dogs, and gratuitously beating up a labourer who was working in the area. The government, deploring 'the great destruction of his Majesty's deer in Waltham Forest by deer stealers who come daily in such numbers' upped the reward for information leading to conviction to £50.

Gradually, the deer-stealers were apprehended, and their identities established for the benefit of both early eighteenth-century law enforcement officers and modern historians. Four of them have a special significance. One was Samuel Gregory, a young man and a blacksmith by trade, who was emerging as a leader, and another was his brother 'Jeremiah', a convicted deer-stealer who had, as we have seen, been acquitted of shooting at Deakins. Then there was Joseph Rose, another convicted deer-stealer who was also found guiltless of any role in the Deakins shooting incident, and, lastly, Mary Brazier, a convicted thief who had met Rose in prison and who had become involved with him, to the extent that her surname in later documentation was sometimes given as Rose. These individuals lay at the centre of an organised body of deer-stealers whose main motivation was simple financial gain. Despite the tendency to romanticise the eighteenth- or nineteenth-century poacher, large-scale poaching, like the deer-stealing that broke out in Waltham Forest in the early 1730s, was essentially geared towards a market for game. The activities of the Gregory brothers and their associates would have been pointless without the existence of contacts that would allow them, either locally or on the London market, to dispose of the deer they stole. One of their local contacts was a young butcher who plied his trade in the area: his name was Richard Turpin.

Piecing together Turpin's early history is difficult. At least we know that he was baptised at Hempstead in Essex, one of a number of boys born to John and Mary Turpin, on 21 September 1705, his parents having been married in the same parish in March 1695. John Turpin (the surname was common in that part of Essex) was a butcher by trade, but also kept a public house at certain points, and it seems likely that his son Richard followed him in both these occupations. There is a tradition, probably erroneous, that he was apprenticed to the butcher's trade in Whitechapel, and another tradition, possibly better founded, that he ran a butcher's shop in Thaxted in Essex for some time. Turpin also married, although there is no surviving parish register entry, and it is impossible to discover the date of the union. The identity of his wife is uncertain, although she was probably an Elizabeth, or Betty, Millington, and she may have been a maidservant when she married. What is certain is that Richard Turpin was a close associate with the Essex deer-stealers.

But by the autumn of 1734 the rump of the Essex deer-stealing gang under the leadership of Samuel Gregory, which had been causing trouble since 1731, had turned to other forms of crime. In January 1735 *The Political State of Great Britain* noted that 'a large gang of rogues have lately associated themselves together, and have committed some very audacious robberies in Essex and other places', the first of these occurring on 29 October 1734 when the shop of Peter Split, a chandler and grocer resident at Woodford in Essex, was raided. Three of the gang went into the shop, called for a half pint of brandy, and were soon joined by first two, and then three more men. 'They had not been long in the shop', the account of the episode continued,

> when one of them pulled out a knife, and then they threatened the master of the house, his wife and daughter with immediate death, if either of them offered to make the least out-cry: while some of them thus stood centuries [sic; i.e., sentries] in the shop, to prevent the family's making any noise, the rest rifled the house of everything of value they could easily carry off; but were so generous as to give back a suit of head cloaths, of about £6 value on the daughter's entreaty, to whom they belonged; there being a sack of meal in the shop, they emptied it on the floor, and put all their plunder therein, and carried it clear off.

Two nights later the same gang, this time eleven in number, carried out another robbery in Woodford, breaking into the house of a gentleman named Wooldridge, 'masked and armed'. They took 'all the brass, pewter, the clock, window curtains, most of the beds and bedding, two fine fowling pieces, and many other things to the value of about £200, and after drinking, or destroying, all his rum, brandy, ale and other liquors, they loaded several horses with their booty, and carried it off'. Turpin was almost certainly involved in at least the first, and probably in the second, of these crimes.

Other robberies followed. On 14 December 1734 four members of the gang, later identified as Samuel Gregory, his brother Jasper, John Jones and John Wheeler, broke into the house of John Gladwin at Chingford, and ransacked the place in the presence of Gladwin and another resident, John Shockley. The list of stolen goods, whose value was limited, suggests that

Gladwin and Shockley were not wealthy men. Five days later, the gang struck in Barking, forcing their way into the home of Ambrose Skinner, a 73-year-old farmer. Evidence given by Skinner told how six men, armed and 'with their faces muffled and disguised', burst into his house and 'pointing their carbines to my breast swore they, if I made any noise or resistance, would immediately put me to death'. Understandably, Skinner thought resistance was pointless, and the intruders removed his garters and tied his hands with them, and then compelled the old man 'to walk about the house with them from one room to another to discover where my money and effects lay, after which they took my purse and keys out of my pocket and therewith attempted to open all the chests and trunks belonging to me'. A maidservant, Elizabeth King, was locked in an upstairs room, while a servant and Skinner's son and his wife, who returned to the house while the robbery was taking place (the raiders were there for three and a half hours), were threatened and bound. Skinner thought that the gang had taken goods and money to the value of £300. Again Turpin was involved in this crime.

The Essex gang's next exploit was an attack on the residence of William Mason, one of the Keepers of Epping Forest, at Hainault Lodge in Essex on 21 December 1734. There was probably a strong element of revenge here: Mason had been involved in the investigation of a number of cases of deer-stealing and robbery over the past few years, and had, in fact, been responsible for the imprisonment of five deer-stealers a year previously. In the 21 December incident, to quote the relevant issue of *The Political State* again, 'no less than fifteen fellows, with their faces blacked, and well armed' were involved. They rushed into Mason's house when his servant opened the door.

Upon hearing the noise, Mr Mason snatched up a blunderbuss and presented it at them; but his wife stepped in between and prevented his firing, fearing they should all be murdered if he killed or hurt any of the rogues; upon this they immediately came up, knocked Mr Mason down, cut him over the head, and bruised him so that he lay dangerously ill for some time; then they rifled the house, where, among other things, they found about 150 guineas in money, after which they packed up all the goods that could be easily carried away, loaded two horses with them, and broke those to pieces they could not carry off, such as tables, chairs, chests of drawers, etc.

One of Mason's servants took advantage of the confusion caused when his master pointed his blunderbuss at the robbers to push through them, to take a horse from his master's stable, and, despite being fired on, to ride away and to rouse the county, returning about two hours later with fifty armed men. By that time, of course, the gang had disappeared. Statements taken from Mason, his wife, his servant Jonathan Richards and others in the household tell slightly different stories: Mason said he could only remember six assailants, while Richards's deposition suggests he escaped on foot rather than on horseback. Yet it remains clear that this was a violent and unpleasant robbery, with the beating of Mason, the attempts to shoot Richards, and the gratuitous destruction of items the gang could not carry away. And yet again the modern reader is struck by the availability of firearms and the ready use that these criminals made of them.

The gang continued with similar robberies in the early months of 1735. They went south of the Thames, and on 11

January 1735 robbed the house of a farmer named Saunders living at Charlton in Kent, the householder again being made to go with the thieves from room to room and tell them where valuables were. A week later five members of the gang, Turpin among them, masked and armed with pistols, ransacked the house of a gentleman named Sheldon living at Croydon in Surrey, taking five sacks of valuables away with them. A robbery involving two men, possibly from the gang, took place at Great Parndon in Essex on 23 January, when the house of a clergyman named Dyde was robbed. Dyde was absent, but his manservant was cut 'in a barbarous manner' about the face. On 1 February a robbery definitely attributable to the Essex gang, by now safely back on home territory, took place at Loughton. The victim was an elderly widow called Shelley. Five men entered her house, menaced her at pistol point, and threatened to 'lay her across the fire' if she did not tell them where her money was. She refused, but her son, who was in the house and unwilling to see his mother tortured, gave the necessary information. The gang found £100, and then stopped to drink wine and ale found in Shelley's cellar, and to cook and eat some meat.

Although the Essex gang's most atrocious offence was yet to come, it is clear from these brief accounts of their crimes that we are not looking at a group of potential folk heroes. These were vicious criminals, with no respect for property or for the right of people to enjoy the safety of their own homes, who had no reservations about using violence, even potentially fatal violence, and who showed considerable brutality towards the elderly. Even today, when it is received wisdom that we are suffering from a unique crime problem, incidents of armed gangs breaking their way into houses whose occupants are present, tying them up, threatening them and possibly torturing them, ransacking their house and breaking up items that are thought to be too difficult to steal are mercifully rare, or are at least still rare enough to shock. Eighteenth-century opinion obviously thought that the activities of this gang were extreme. One of those who played an active part in attempting to track the gang down and identify its members was Martin Bladen, an Essex justice of the peace. Bladen took depositions from the gang's victims, and in late December 1734 sent a file of these documents up to Earl Tylney, Lord Warden of Waltham Forest, asking for them to be brought to the attention of one of the Secretaries of State. Bladen expressed the opinion that 'unless his Majesty shall be graciously pleased, to interpose his authority, for the discovery of these outrageous practices, the common course of law, will prove an insufficient barrier, for the lives and fortunes of his good subjects'. Bladen also noted that 'the terror these robberies have struck into the country people especially the wealthy farmers, is incredible; and your Lordship cannot do an act of greater charity, than to endeavour to deliver them out of it'.

Bladen was convinced that the two Woodford robberies, and the robberies at Skinner's and Mason's houses, were all carried out by the same gang, and as the robberies continued into 1735 the newspapers habitually attributed them to the same group of criminals. However, both contemporary observers and later popular historians have been a little too ready in attributing criminal acts to coherent and tightly organised gangs. Even so, it is possible to list the main members of what the newspapers of 1734–5 described as the Essex gang, and what is generally known among modern writers as the Gregory gang. At its centre lay the three Gregory brothers: Samuel, the leader, Jasper and Jeremy. There was Thomas Rowden, aged about thirty, a pewterer by trade, who had been tried and acquitted of counter-feiting coin in 1733. There was William Saunders or Saunder-son. There was Joseph Rose, aged about forty, another former blacksmith and a convicted deer-stealer, and his partner Mary Brazier. There was John Fielder, John Jones, a Hackney resi-dent, Humphrey Walker, aged about fifty, Herbert Haines, aged about twenty-five, a barber or periwig-maker turned thief, and Richard Turpin, the butcher turned robber. And there was the youngest member of the gang, a youth aged between fifteen and seventeen named John Wheeler.

By early 1735 the gang members were all resident in Lon-don, demonstrating the accuracy of Henry Fielding's claims that the capital provided a unique place of refuge for criminals, and also demonstrating how important organised crime was becoming in London's life. Turpin lived in Whitechapel, with Thomas Rowden and Jasper Gregory living nearby in the Rad-cliff Highway area, a notoriously dangerous district. Samuel Gregory lived with Jasper, Jeremy Gregory and William Saun-ders lived in Clerkenwell, and Herbert Haines in Shoreditch. Joseph Rose, Mary Brazier and John Wheeler lived in Dawes Street in Westminster, Humphrey Walker was also resident in Westminster, while John Fielder lived in the same area. One suspects that, for the most part, the gang members chose land-lords who were not over-scrupulous about the character of those to whom they rented accommodation. As far as the gang mem-bers were concerned, being based in London made the gather-ing of information about possible victims easier, and it also allowed the gang to operate on the wide arc of the metropolitan area's fringes. Gang members involved in each specific crime met together at inns before they struck.

Thus it was in the early afternoon of 4 February 1735 Samuel Gregory, Richard Turpin, John Wheeler, Joseph Rose and John Fielder gathered together in the Black Horse Inn in the Broadway, Westminster (landlord John Bowler), close to where Wheeler and Rose, who were regular drinkers there, lived. The five were planning to carry out a robbery at the house of a farmer named Joseph Lawrence of Earlsbury Farm in Edgware: Samuel Gregory had worked in the area in his earlier incarnation as a blacksmith, and thought that the pickings would be substantial, as Lawrence's habit of paying his workers good wages had convinced Gregory that the farmer was a rich man. At about 4.15 that afternoon they stopped for a drink at an inn near to their target, and, after stopping at another inn for beer and bacon and eggs, they finally came to Lawrence's house. They approached on foot, captured and bound a shepherd boy named James Emmerton, and then, in their accustomed manner, burst into the house armed with pistols. Joseph Lawrence, a manservant called John Pate, and a maidservant named Dorothy Street were in the house. The two servants were bound and placed in a room with young Emmerton, then Joseph Lawrence was threatened with death should he not reveal where his money was. The house was ransacked brutally, and Lawrence himself, a man aged more than seventy, was very roughly handled. His breeches were pulled round his ankles to shackle them, and he was dragged round the house while the gang asked where his money and valuables were. He refused to give this information, so Turpin beat his bare buttocks until they were severely bruised, and the other gang members beat the old

Behold the Villains dire disgrace!
Not Death itself can end.
He finds no peaceful Burial Place,
His breathless Corse no friend.

Torn from the Root, that wicked Tongue,
Which dayly swore and curst!
Those Eyeballs, from their Sockets wrung,
That glow'd with lawless Lust!

His Heart expos'd to prying Eyes,
To Pity has no Claim
But dreadful! from his Bones shall rise,
His Monument of Shame.

7. The dissection of the body of an executed criminal in an anatomy theatre, again depicted by Hogarth, as The Reward of Cruelty in his 'The Four Stages of Cruelty' series of 1751. Had the York mob not intervened, this would have been the fate of Turpin's body (University of York Library).

man about the head with their pistols. A kettle of water was emptied over his head, and he was sat bare-buttocked on the fire in an effort to make him talk. After this he was pulled round the house alternatively by his nose or by his hair by Fielder, Rose and Turpin.

Samuel Gregory found diversion elsewhere. He led the maidservant, Dorothy Street, upstairs, ostensibly to force her to divulge where her master's money was. In fact, he took her into a garret and raped her at pistol point, threatening to kill her if she did not give in (her hands were still tied). When he had finished with her, Gregory let her go downstairs, where she appeared weeping. Asked by Wheeler if she had been beaten, she replied, 'No, but one of your men has lain with me.' The gang vacillated about robbing the house of Lawrence's son, also called Joseph, which was nearby, but eventually decided against it. They put what they had found in old Joseph Lawrence's house into sacks or into their pockets, and rode off. The value of the stolen goods was less than thirty pounds.

The events at Earlsbury Farm on the evening of 4 February must finally end any desire that the modern reader might feel to romanticise the historical Richard Turpin. Here is a man capable of torturing a seventy-year-old in a brutal fashion, a man who was happy to work in a gang with criminal associates like Samuel Gregory who could rape a servant girl at pistol point. Yet there was one more incident where a solid family were to be terrorised in their own home by the Essex gang. Three days later, on 7 February, Samuel Gregory, Richard Turpin, John Wheeler, Joseph Rose, John Fielder, William Saunders and Humphrey Walker set out to raid another farm, in this instance one owned by William Francis at Marylebone. Two servants working outside the house were attacked and tied up, as was William Francis when he wandered into the stable where they were being held. The gang, as ever armed with pistols, then burst into the house, beat Francis's wife about the head with the butt of a whip until blood ran down her face, and also beat her daughter and a maidservant, tied them up, and then began their usual practices of ransacking the house and threatening violence if they were not told where money was hidden. The seven made off with just under ninety pounds' worth of goods and money: among the goods were such family treasures as a coral for a child set in silver, a gold mourning ring, and a gold ring bearing the words 'God did decree our unity'. Modern victims of burglary and robbery will know how much the experience of the break-in, and the loss of goods valued far above their intrinsic worth, certainly far above what Mary Brazier would be able to fence them for, must have shattered the domestic life of the Francis household, as it must have done with the Lawrences, and with so many of the Essex gang's other victims. But by now time had almost run out for this particular group of unpleasant thugs.

The day after the Francis robbery, 8 February 1735, the Duke of Newcastle issued yet another proclamation, offering a reward of £50 for information leading to the conviction of the 'several persons' concerned in the two Woodford robberies, and the robberies at widow Shelley and the Reverend Dyde's houses. Strong incentives for finding the robbers were now on offer, but it was a chance coincidence involving an unusually observant innkeeper that enabled Nemesis to descend on Samuel Gregory and his associates.

It will be remembered that on their way to carry out the Earlsbury Farm robbery Samuel Gregory, Turpin, Wheeler, Rose and Fielder stopped to drink at two alehouses in Edgware. One of these was the Nine Pins and Bowl, its landlord being Richard Wood. On 11 February 1735 Wood, on business in London, was walking down King Street in Bloomsbury when he saw some horses standing outside an alehouse door that he recognised as being among the horses used by the five strangers who had drunk at his inn the night his neighbour Joseph Lawrence had been robbed. Once more, a contemporary journal reports what happened:

> Upon this he called a constable, and getting some other assis-
> tants, they went into the alehouse, where the horses were stand-
> ing, in which they found a woman [probably Mary Brazier]
> drinking punch with three fellows, whom Mr Wood immedi-
> ately knew to be three of the five fellows who had been at his
> house, upon which the constable and his assistants laid hold of
> the company, and, after some resistance, they were secured, and
> five pistols taken from them. They were immediately taken
> before justice Hind, in Great Ormond Street, where they
> declared their names to be John Fielder, Joseph Rose [in fact
> William Saunders], and John Wheeler, but obstinately denied
> that they had been concerned in robbing Mr Laurence, or any
> other robbery: however, the justice most prudently signed their
> *Mittimus* to New Prison, on suspicion.

As so often with the Turpin story, there is a slightly different version of this episode, which attributes the discovery of Fielder, Saunders and Wheeler to a servant of Joseph Lawrence's, and names the inn as the Punch Bowl on King Street. Interestingly, both Lawrence's son Thomas and John Pate, Lawrence's servant, were subsequently to depose that they were present when the prisoners were taken, and it is difficult to see their presence as coincidental. One suspects that they were making a search for the robbers in central London, that Wood knew this, and was only too happy to ensure that information about his discovery reached them as quickly as possible.

All sources agree on what happened next. John Wheeler was the youngest of the gang, maybe as young as fifteen, and he obviously took the experience of being arrested rather less phlegmatically than the more hardened Fielder and Saunders. As the journal report continues, Wheeler probably 'began to foresee, that they would be discovered, and sufficient proofs found against them, before they could get out of jail', and accordingly told the constable who had arrested them 'that if he would carry him back to the justice he would confess, and inform against the whole gang'. The constable took him back to Hind, to whom he 'made an ample confession of all the robberies they had committed'. Upon this Fielder and Saunders were committed to Newgate, and Wheeler was sent to the New Prison for a lengthy period of what was in effect protective custody, punctuated by trips out to give evidence at the trials of his erstwhile associates.

On Monday 17 February three more of the gang, Joseph Rose, Mary Brazier and Humphrey Walker, were taken, like those captured on 11 February, while drinking punch, in this instance at a chandler's shop. The shop stood in the appropriately named Thieving Lane, where the trio had arrived from their previous base the Friday before, their desire for new lodgings obviously sharpened by the capture of Fielder, Saunders and Wheeler. The nine-strong party that made the arrest was headed by a constable, Archelaus Pullen, but it is probably no coincidence that it included Joseph Lawrences's two sons and his servant John Pate: the Lawrence boys and their father's servant were clearly out to obtain vengeance for what had happened to Lawrence senior and his household. Rose and Walker were armed, and resisted. One of those aiding Pullen, Richard Bartram, deposed that Rose pointed a pistol at his breast, and pulled the trigger, but that he was able get his finger between the hammer and the lock and prevented it from firing, while Walker tried to pull a pistol that became entangled in his pocket, and was knocked down by a hackney coachman named Harrowfield. Pullen and his associates found two trunks of stolen goods in the suspects' lodgings, and they were duly taken to the Gatehouse, Westminster, and examined by a justice, Nathaniel Blackerby, the next day; farmer Francis's daughter, Sarah, and the maidservant Eleanor Williams were there to identify some of the stolen goods. Mary Brazier remained in the Gatehouse for further questioning, while Rose and Walker were committed to Newgate.

Wheeler continued to give information against his former associates, and a statement, which was eventually completed on Thursday 20 February, opened the way for the next set of arrests. The details that appeared in the press of the period implicated those members of the Essex gang who had not so far been apprehended in specific offences, and also gives some idea of what Samuel Gregory, Dick Turpin and their associates looked like. John Jones, 'a carpenter by trade, about five and a half feet high, fresh coloured, pock holes in his face and wears a brown wig', was implicated in the robbery at Gladwin's house at Chingford. Four others were 'charged upon oath for committing several robberies in Essex, Middlesex, Surrey and Kent. The first of these was Samuel Gregory, 'about five feet seven inches high, has a scar about an inch and a half long on his right cheek, is fresh coloured wears a brown wig and is 23 years old is a smith or farrier by trade'. Then came Thomas Rowden, 'a little man, well set, fresh coloured and full faced, has small pockholes in his face, wears a blue grey coat with a light wig, a pewterer by trade', aged about thirty years. The third was Herbert Haines, a barber or periwig maker keeping a shop in Hog Lane in Shoreditch, 'about five feet seven inches high, of a pale complexion, wears a brown wig and a brick coloured cloth coat, aged about 24 years'. And lastly came 'Richard Turpin, a butcher by trade, is a tall fresh coloured man, very much marked with the small pox, about 26 years of age, about five feet nine inches high, lived some time ago in Whitechapel and did lately lodge somewhere about Millbank, Westminster, wears a blue grey coat and a natural wig'.

Rose, Fielder, Saunders and Walker were tried at the Middlesex General Session held between 26 February and 1 March 1735. The full quartet were indicted on separate counts of burglary and robbery at the houses of William Francis and Joseph Lawrence, while Fielder, Rose and Walker were indicted for burgling the house of Ambrose Skinner. Richard Turpin and Samuel Gregory, although as yet unapprehended, were also named on some of the indictments. The four members of the gang who had been captured were all capitally convicted, and their hangings scheduled for 10 March. Humphrey Walker died in Newgate in the early hours of that day: at the age of fifty he was the eldest of the gang, and had probably been badly beaten in the course of his arrest. Fielder, Rose and Saunders, together with the other ten felons who had been condemned to hang that day, and escorted by a company of foot guards appointed to forestall any rescue attempt, were taken from the prison a few hours later and driven off to be executed at Tyburn, the three members of the Essex gang sharing the same cart. After they were dead, their bodies were cut down, and taken to Edgware, where they were hung in chains on gibbets until they rotted, grim reminders of the enormity of the Earlsbury Farm robbery, and of the fate of criminals who committed such heinous offences. And, coincidentally, some miles to the east one of their former colleagues was sentenced to death on 10 March. At the Essex assizes at Chelmsford Jasper Gregory, who had been apprehended before the capture of Fielder, Saunders and Wheeler, was indicted on two counts, for a highway robbery committed against a man called Giles Cory, and for his part in the robbery at John Gladwin's house in Chingford. He was executed three weeks later.

Despite the fate of several of their associates, the surviving gang members continued to commit crimes in February and March, offences possibly including a number of robberies in Essex and one at Brockley in Kent. On 7 April two core members of the gang, Samuel and Jeremy Gregory, committed a crime too many. They had gone south of London, to Shoreham and Brighton, and then journeyed on to Southampton, hoping to take a boat to Guernsey, but found they had insufficient money for their passage. They therefore made their way back to London, and en route, on Milford Heath near Godalming, robbed Sir John Osborne, stealing a gold watch and a considerable amount of money from him. They also attempted to rob a man called Spooner, landlord of the Red Lion inn at Guildford, who escaped, despite being fired on by the two brothers. A day or two after, the Gregorys attended a cockfight near Petersfield, and attention was drawn to them when Samuel Gregory's coat accidentally came open, and a pistol was seen stuck in his belt. Local gossip connected this incident with the robbing of Sir John Osborne, and the pair were soon traced to an alehouse at Rake near Petersfield. Four local men, armed with a motley collection of pistols, swords and scythes, went to apprehend them. The brothers, after at first going along with the arrest, pulled pistols from under the pillows of the bed they had been sharing, and in the following mêlée Samuel Gregory was injured in the face by a sword, losing the tip of his nose, and Jeremy was shot in the thigh. The pair were taken to a justice of the peace, and committed to Winchester gaol. Osborne went to confront the two men, and Samuel Gregory confessed his identity, and to being a participant in the Earlsbury robbery.

Jeremy Gregory died of his wounds in Winchester gaol, the exact date of his death being unknown. Samuel was taken to London on 13 May 1735, handcuffed and with his feet chained under the belly of the horse on which he rode, and guarded by seven or eight men. He was first taken to the New Prison, where Wheeler swore that Gregory had been involved in the Earlsbury robbery, and was subsequently transferred to Newgate under a strong guard. He was tried at the Old Bailey on 22 May 1735 on six counts, including the rape of Dorothy Street, for the theft of a horse of Thomas Humphrey, and for burglary and robbery at the houses of Joseph Lawrence and William Francis. He was found guilty on all six indictments and sentenced to death. He was executed on 4 June, his body later being sent to hang in chains alongside the rotting remains of his three former confederates at Edgware. Shortly after the Gregory brothers had been taken down in Hampshire, another member of the gang, Herbert Haines, the barber or periwig-maker, was also captured. He had, for some time, been having an affair with a married woman, the wife of a John Carroll with whom Haines had previously worked as a journeyman. Haines went to Gravesend with the woman, intending that they should set sail together for Holland in a sloop called the *Chandos*. This was too much of a humiliation for Carroll, who informed Henry Palmer, a local constable. Palmer boarded the sloop and apprehended Haines and his consort. Despite offers from both Haines and an apparently remorseful Carroll of a £50 bribe to let Haines escape, Palmer, accompanied by a James Freeland, took the suspect to London, where he was handed over to a justice of the peace and committed to Newgate. Transferred to Chelmsford on 18 May to stand trial at the Essex summer assizes, he was sentenced to death, and executed there on 8 August 1735, apparently meeting his end with a quiet dignity.

In was in April, the month that saw the arrests of Samuel and Jeremy Gregory and Henry Haines, that Mary Brazier was tried at the Old Bailey, and sentenced to fourteen years' transportation to America. It took time to gather enough transportees to make the process worth the while for the contractor responsible for shipping them across the Atlantic, and Brazier did not leave England until December. And it was in that month that one of the few of the gang members still at large, John Jones, was taken. Jones had left his native area, Hackney, and gone into hiding after the first 'discoveries' of Wheeler. But the lure of his home town proved too strong, and he returned late in 1735. His arrival did not go unremarked, and a man named Dison Green, hearing that John Jones was back in Hackney, went with another man called Francis Francis to the local constable, Nicholas Graves; the trio then went to the house where Jones was staying and arrested him. The justice of the peace they took him to was Henry Norris, whom we encountered in the previous chapter. The two men, according to Norris's notebook, 'do severally voluntarily say that John Jones late of Homerton is publicly reputed to have been an accomplice in several notorious late robberies in this and other counties & that they do believe the same to be true'. Jones 'denied his having been concerned in any ill deed', but Norris committed him to Newgate on suspicion of felony. In March 1736 he was transferred to Chelmsford, where he was tried for his participation in the burglary and robbery of the house of John Gladwin in Chingford. He was found guilty, sentenced to death, and then reprieved to await transportation. He eventually sailed for America in December 1736, a year after Mary Brazier.

There is an entrenched tendency to disparage eighteenth-century law enforcement, operating as it did before the modern system of professional police forces, prisons, probation officers and social workers came into place. This tendency has grown into a full-blown historical myth that would dismiss the law enforcement system of eighteenth-century England as being inefficient and characterised by 'sanguinary chaos'. Yet the breaking of the Essex gang constitutes a remarkable triumph for eighteenth-century crime-control practices. In February 1735 the Essex gang was a feared, successful, and anonymous grouping of organised criminals. By the end of that year it had been smashed. Obviously, young John Wheeler's snap decision to turn King's evidence was crucial, and payments recorded in Treasury accounts also suggest that the prospect of a reward did much to motivate those involved in the capture of the various gang members. Yet it must have taken more than the prospect of a reward to encourage members of the public to take on armed and desperate criminals, while the much-maligned parish constables of the period also seem to have done well in detecting criminals or acting promptly on receipt of information that they were in the area.

So by the end of December the bodies of Samuel Gregory, John Fielder, Joseph Rose and William Saunders were rotting on gibbets at Edgware, near the location of their most notorious crime. Jasper Gregory and Herbert Haines had been hanged at Chelmsford. Humphrey Walker and Jeremy Gregory had died in gaol, the first at Newgate, the second at Winchester. Mary Brazier was setting out to undergo fourteen years' penal servitude in America, while John Jones was in prison, awaiting transfer to Essex and the trial that would send him in the same direction a year later. John Wheeler was still being held, probably for his own safety as much as for any other reason, in the New Prison.

And that left Thomas Rowden and Richard Turpin.

It was at this stage that Richard Turpin finally turned to the activity for which he was to achieve lasting fame, highway robbery. On

10 and 12 April there were robberies at Mile End and Epping Forest that were carried out by three men thought to be Turpin, Rowden, and the as yet uncaptured John Jones. Highway robbery was unusually rife in the spring and summer of 1735 (there was a proclamation, dated 15 July of that year, which complained of the prevalence of highwaymen and street robbers and upped the rewards against them) and it is impossible to state with any precision which of the robberies carried out around London were attributable to this trio, or, after Jones's arrest, to Turpin and Rowden. On 10 July, however, came the first robbery in which the press identified them as the perpetrators.

> Last Thursday night about eight o'clock Mr Vane of Richmond, and Mr. James Bradford of the Borough of Southwark, going from thence to Richmond were attacked between Wandsworth and Barns Common by two highwaymen supposed to be Turpin the butcher, and Rowden the pewterer, the remaining two of Gregory's gang who robbed them of their money &c, dismounted them, made them pull of their horses' bridles, then turning them adrift they rode off towards Roehampton where a gentleman was robb'd, as is supposed, by the same highwaymen, of a watch, and about £3 4s in money.

Four days later they struck again in the same area, when they robbed a Mr Omar of Southwark. Turpin thought Omar knew him, and apparently had to be dissuaded by Rowden from shooting him. The next day a proclamation was published, adding £100 to the already existing rewards on offer to anybody giving information bringing either of the two men to conviction. This was a considerable incentive.

Turpin and Rowden carried out a number of robberies over the second half of 1735. At first they operated mainly in the Barnes Common area, so that by August, as the *London Evening Post* for 30 August–2 September was to report, the inhabitants of Putney, Roehampton, Barnes and the surrounding parishes were raising, by subscription, their own reward funds 'for encouragement of such as shall take, or cause to be taken, any persons who have or shall commit robberies on the highway'. But by this time they were already ranging more widely, with, for example, two robberies carried out on the Hertfordshire side of the capital reported in the *London Evening Post* of 2–4 September. The duo's increasing reputation, and perhaps their growing recklessness, was signalled when the same journal, in its issue of 9–11 October, reported that Turpin and Rowden had shown 'the insolence to ride through the City at Noon-Day'. But by about this time the two highwaymen seem to have put a stop to their activities. The most likely explanation is that the apprehension of John Jones reminded them that they were not invulnerable, and that they decided to quit both highway robbery and the London area for a while.

What Rowden did next is well documented. Before he had joined the Essex gang he had been tried for counterfeiting coin, and he went to Gloucestershire and resumed this activity, calling himself Daniel Crispe. In July 1736 he was committed to Gloucester gaol under that name on two counts of passing counterfeit coin, in much the same way as Turpin was to be committed to York Castle just over two years later as the suspected horse-thief John Palmer. Although counterfeiting coin was a capital offence, passing counterfeit money was not, and Rowden, alias Daniel Crispe, was fined and imprisoned for a year. While he was serving his time in Gloucester gaol he fell to drinking with a man who had come to visit a friend there. Rowden asked the man to pass Daniel Crispe's compliments on to a mutual acquaintance. The two men met, but when Rowden's drinking companion passed the message on, the third party declared that he knew no Daniel Crispe who had been convicted for passing counterfeit coin, but that he did know a Thomas Rowden who had been in trouble for counterfeiting. When the other insisted that the incarcerated man was called Daniel Crispe, Rowden's acquaintance went to Gloucester gaol, and had Daniel Crispe pointed out to him. Recognising him as Thomas Rowden, he rode to London, and informed a magistrate that he knew of Rowden's whereabouts. He was advised to inform a magistrate in Gloucestershire; this was done, and Rowden was sent down to stand trial in Essex for his part in the Ambrose Skinner robbery. He was tried on 20 July 1737, and was found guilty and sentenced to be hanged. But the judge recommended him for transportation, and he eventually sailed for Virginia on 9 June 1738. By that date another major figure in our story had left the scene. John Wheeler had died, almost certainly of natural causes, at Hackney in January 1738, and was buried in St John's churchyard there. He had been released from the New Prison in September 1736. The prison keeper, Thomas Cavanagh, claimed £30 1s., or a shilling a day, for his board and lodging for the 601 days he had been incarcerated.

While the fates of the other members of the now-shattered Essex gang are well documented, the central figure in the story disappears from the historical record at this point. Although the evidence is equivocal, it seems virtually certain that this disappearance was because Turpin made his way to Holland at the

end of 1735. There were a number of reported sightings of him
there, although none of them are fully reliable, and, since
Turpin proved himself able to go to ground under an assumed
identity in Yorkshire and Lincolnshire for a lengthy period
before the discoveries of February 1739, it is not impossible that,
like Rowden, he simply disappeared into provincial life after
John Jones was apprehended. Certainly, it was to the advantage
of the authorities to give support to the notion that Turpin had
left the country: not being able to catch a Turpin living in Holland was considerably less embarrassing than not being able to
catch a Turpin living in England. But the manner in which
Turpin did re-enter the historical record suggests that he was
back in England and was resuming his career as a highwayman
early in 1737.

On 12 February of that year the newspapers reported that
Turpin's wife Elizabeth, her maid Hannah Elcombe, and a
man called Robert Nott had been committed to Hertford gaol.
They had spent all night with Turpin at Puckeridge in Hertfordshire, but Turpin had made his escape and ridden off
towards Cambridge. The Hertford assize records show that the
three were committed to Hertford gaol 'on a violent suspicion of
being dangerous rogues and robbing upon the highway', but
when they came to trial on 28 February the two women were
acquitted, although Nott was held until he could find sureties to
appear at the next sessions. Turpin again disappears from the
historical record for a month after the Puckeridge incident, and
on his reappearance was working with two other highwaymen,
Matthew King and Stephen Potter. The trio may have operated
in Leicestershire for a while, but by the end of April they were
back in the London area.

On 29 April one of the gang, variously reported as King or Turpin, stole a horse named Whitestockings, the property of Joseph Major, close to the Green Man Inn at Leytonstone. Joseph Major went to the Green Man, and reported his loss to the landlord, Richard Bayes, who was to become an early biographer of Turpin. By now the gang was based in London, and rode into town and stabled the stolen horse at the Red Lion Inn in Whitechapel. Bayes put out enquiries about the whereabouts of Whitestockings, presumably through a network of contacts in the licensed victualling trade, and quickly received information that a horse similar to the one reported to have been stolen was being kept at the Red Lion. Bayes recruited some assistants, and went to the Red Lion on Monday 1 May, where he and his associates waited in the stables for somebody to come for the horse. King's brother John eventually turned up, was apprehended, and taken into the inn for questioning. His claims that he had bought the horse were not believed, and he was reported to a constable. John King, clearly frightened, said that there was a man waiting for the horse in Red Lion Street, and Bayes, going outside, saw the man and recognised him as Matthew King.

Bayes tried to apprehend him, whereupon, in Bayes's version of the event

King immediately drew a pistol, which he clapped to Mr Bayes' breast; but it luckily flash'd in the pan; upon which King struggling to get out his other, it had twisted round his pocket and he could not. Turpin, who was waiting not far off on horseback, hearing a skirmish, came up, when King cried out 'Dick, shoot him, or we are taken by G-d', at which instant Turpin fir'd his pistol, and it mist [i.e. missed] Mr Bayes, and shot King in two places, who cried out; 'Dick, you have killed me', which Turpin hearing, he rode away as hard as he could. King fell at the shot, though he liv'd a week after and gave Turpin the character of a coward.

According to Bayes, King gave information that Turpin would have ridden to 'a noted house by Hackney Marsh'. Further enquiries revealed that Turpin had indeed visited the house, and that he had sworn revenge on Bayes, saying, 'I have lost the best fellow-man I ever had in my life; I shot poor King in endeavouring to kill that dog.'

One suspects that Bayes's story of Turpin swearing revenge against him is at best heavily embellished, and interestingly, within a few days of the incident the newspapers were reporting that it was Bayes, not Turpin, who had shot King. Convincing King that it was Turpin who shot him (the shooting obviously took place in a confused mêlée) would have had the effect, successfully achieved if we can trust Bayes's account, of making King give information about his colleague, while if the story spread it would also help make Bayes a less likely target for the vengeance of King's relatives or associates. There are a number of contemporary reports of the incident, each of them giving different emphases in their account of what happened in Red Lion Street on the night of 1–2 May 1737. What strikes the modern reader again is how this incident provides yet more evidence of the easy use which both criminals and those setting out to capture them made of firearms. The firearms, especially the pistols of the period, were mercifully frequently ineffective, but on this occasion fatal wounds had been inflicted. Matthew

King the highwayman, as Bayes reported, indeed died a few days later, after having given some interesting information about his criminal activities with Turpin and Potter.

Turpin headed for Epping Forest, which he, King and Potter had used as a hiding place in the recent past. Epping Forest provided no real security for Turpin. He had a hiding place in the forest in the form of a cave, which several accounts suggest was stocked with a bed, some food and part of a bottle of wine, and clean shirts. But he was seen by Thomas Morris, servant to Mr Thompson, one of the Keepers of the Forest. Morris, rather rashly, decided to capture Turpin (some reports suggest that he was accompanied by another man) and late in the evening of 4 May came upon him near to his hiding place. Accounts of what happened next vary. The *London Evening Post*, for example, suggests that Morris approached Turpin alone, confident that Turpin would only be armed with pistols, and that the gun he had borrowed would outrange him if it came to shooting. Turpin, unhappily for his would-be apprehender, had a carbine with which he shot Morris, who died instantly. The *Political State* had Morris, accompanied by an anonymous higgler, take Turpin by the collar, and tell him he was under arrest, whereupon Turpin shot him with a pistol. Bayes, in his biography of Turpin, gives yet a third version, incorporating the unnamed higgler but having Turpin shoot Morris with a carbine after talking to him and lulling him into a false sense of security. One thing is certain: Turpin shot and killed Thomas Morris. He had, finally, added murder to the tally of his crimes.

Turpin's movements immediately after the murder are unclear. There were a number of reports of his committing further robberies in the London area in early May, but their authenticity remains unproved; one newspaper report, showing more sense than many, commented that on Tuesday 10 May 'a single highwayman robbed four coaches and several passengers at different times on Hounslow Heath and they gave out it was Turpin, but that fellow having done so much mischief of late, runs in everybody's head'. This newspaper did, however, add an illuminating comment:

> The people about Epping Forest say he will never be taken till a proclamation is published offering a reward for apprehending of him and give the reason, that as he had declared he will never be taken alive but he will kill, or be killed, and it will be dangerous to attempt it, and if they should take him he'll be tried for the murder of Thompson's man and if convicted of that, the persons that apprehend him will be entitled to no reward unless there's a proclamation, which makes them backward in endeavouring to take him.

This throws interesting light both on Turpin's standing as somebody who was thought to be a desperate offender, and also on the importance of the prospect of a reward in helping encourage the public to bring such an offender in. And, of course, on 25 June 1737, possibly after it was clear that Turpin was not going to be captured in the immediate aftermath of the Morris killing, Newcastle issued a proclamation, stating that because of the murder of Morris and 'several notorious felonies and robberies' which Turpin had committed, a reward of £200 was offered 'to any person or persons who shall discover the said criminal, so as he may be apprehended and convicted as afore٬ said, to be paid upon such conviction, over and above all other rewards to which the said person or persons may otherwise be entitled'. By this time Turpin was beginning the journey which would bring him to Long Sutton in Lincolnshire in the early summer of 1737, via Brough in Yorkshire. Even before the reward had been offered, Turpin had realised that the south was far too hot for him.

The proclamation of 25 June also gives us the fullest description we have of Turpin: 'About thirty years of age, by trade a butcher, about five feet nine inches high, of a brown complexion, very much marked with the small pox, his cheek bones broad, his face thinner toward the bottom, his visage short, pretty upright, and broad about the shoulders.' There is no reliable contemporary portrait of Turpin: he was simply not important enough a figure for that.

What does survive are materials from which it is possible to construct an outline of his criminal career. Turpin was a hard man capable of acts of cruelty, who had an uncertain temper and was prone to violence, who had no reservations, by the end of his career, about using firearms, and who also, far from being the daredevil of later fiction, knew when the best policy was to cut and run. Despite the later mythologising, he comes across as an unpleasant man, albeit for a short period a successful and notorious criminal, whose offences ran from robbery with vio-lence to murder. Going back to the contemporary record, and ignoring the later myths, provides a rather unexpected Turpin, yet one whose descendants, as we read reports of crime in our own newspapers, are still very much with us. One wonders if, three centuries into the future, any of our modern criminals will be candidates for romanticisation.

And, finally, there is a point of detail to register. The

contemporary records, the newspaper reports, court archives and official documents of the 1730s, are resoundingly silent about two of the key elements in the modern construction of Turpin: there is no mention of the ride to York, and no mention that Turpin ever owned a horse named Black Bess. Not only was Dick Turpin clearly failing to qualify at the time of his death as the stuff legends are made of, but two of the main components of his later legend were simply not being attached to him. That we now consider Black Bess and the ride to York as essential parts of the Turpin legend, and, indeed, the fact that the Turpin legend exists at all, was due to a powerful fictional recreation of Turpin that occurred nearly a century after his execution and, perhaps not entirely coincidentally, at the precise point at which highway robbery in its classic form had ceased to be a threat to the law-abiding. To understand how this happened, we need to set Turpin aside for a while, and turn to the life of a once eminent, but now more or less forgotten, figure.

chapter *five*

THE MAN *from* MANCHESTER

Manchester was regarded by many early nineteenth-century observers as symbolising the massive, and not universally welcome, transition to modernity which was perceived to be occurring in the half-century after 1800. There was the onset of mass urbanisation; the arrival of the novel phenomenon of factory production; the rise of an industrial bourgeoisie that challenged the traditional landed aristocracy; and, perhaps most disturbing of all in the wake of the French Revolution, the emergence of a large, and potentially politically conscious, industrial proletariat. It was at St Peter's Fields in Manchester that, on 16 August 1819, one of the most notorious episodes in British labour history happened, when tragic mismanagement by the local authorities in their attempts to disperse a large but orderly and peaceable political demonstration resulted in eleven deaths and hundreds of injuries. Unforgotten and unforgiven for generations, the event passed into history, in a bitter parody of Wellington's great victory of four years earlier, as the Peterloo Massacre. And, less than thirty years after the Peterloo Massacre, Friedrich Engels, a young German working in his father's textile business, used his observations of the appalling living conditions of mill operatives and other workers in the city as the basis of that key text of the Marxist canon, *The Condition of the Working Class in England*, first published in Leipzig in 1845.

The transformations that underlay the Peterloo Massacre and the writings of Engels and other commentators were, to contemporaries, not only deep but also disturbingly rapid. In 1772 there were 25,000 people living in Manchester; by 1840 there were 260,000 in the Manchester–Salford conurbation. In 1786 the visitor to Manchester would have seen only one factory chimney, that belonging to the mill owned by Richard Ark-wright; by 1816 there were eighty-two steam powered textile factories in Manchester and Salford. Small wonder that many contemporaries regarded Manchester as the prototype for a new world of factory production, urbanisation and incipient class politics. Small wonder likewise that later historians were to dub Manchester the 'shock city' of the Industrial Revolution.

'As you enter Manchester from the Rusholme', wrote a commentator of 1848, 'the town at the lower end of Oxford Road has the appearance of one dense volume of smoke, more forbidding than the entrance to Dante's inferno. It struck me that were it not for previous knowledge, no man would have the courage to enter it.' Half a century earlier, Manchester had not assumed so alarming an aspect, but it was already a place experiencing massive expansion and change. Thus John Aiken, who published a description of the Manchester area in 1795, commented:

> The new streets built within these few years have nearly doubled the size of the town. Most of them are wide and spacious, with excellent and large houses, principally of brick made on the spot ... As Manchester may bear comparison with the metro-

polis itself in the rapidity with which whole new streets have been raised, and in its extension on every side towards the surrounding country; so it unfortunately vies with, or exceeds the metropolis, in the closeness with which the poor are crowded in offensive, dark, damp and incommodious habitations, a too fertile source of disease!

Yet at the time when Aiken wrote, Manchester's status as the shock city of the Industrial Revolution still lay in the future. Despite the expansion and the early signs of factory production, the centre of Manchester, with its many fine Georgian houses, still had the air of a traditional if prosperous eighteenth-century town, while Manchester's elite consisted not of the cotton merchants who were to become predominant as the nineteenth century progressed, but rather a mixture of merchants and the representatives of the more traditional professions, many of them from long-established families that had strong links with the surrounding countryside.

One such family was the Ainsworths. They had prospered over the generations, and in time raised themselves into the ranks of the local gentry, in particular acquiring an attractive property at Spotland Gate. One of them, Thomas, in 1802 married Ann, the daughter of the Reverend Ralph Harrison, minister of the Unitarian chapel in Cross Street. Harrison was a noted scholar and tutor, a gifted musician who also had a keen sense for business, making a fortune of £60,000 from land speculations. The union between Thomas Ainsworth and Ann Harrison produced two children, both boys. The first of these, William Harrison Ainsworth, was born at the parental home, 21 King Street, Manchester, on 4 February 1805.

On his own later account, William's childhood was a happy one. He had, apparently, a good relationship with his father. Thomas Ainsworth was a cultured and educated man, who also had a taste for local legends and romantic tales, and who would frequently sit his son on his knee and tell him adventure stories. He was especially fond, according to his son's later memories, of tales about highwaymen, and in particular Ainsworth claimed that these stories generated an early interest in Dick Turpin. The tales of highwaymen and other romantic figures were often acted out by William and his friends. Young William also picked up a sense of local legends and local history, and became particularly interested in the impact of the Jacobite rebellions in Lancashire, spending time talking to people who could remember the local ramifications of Bonnie Prince Charlie's rising of 1745. He received a more formal education at Manchester Grammar School, which he entered in 1817, and then, in 1822, went to work in his father's law firm, learning conveyancing.

From the start, and to his father's occasional despair, it was obvious that William's heart was not in the study and practice of the law. He was far more interested in literature, an interest that was reinforced by the presence in his father's firm of James Crossley, a young man five years William's senior who had come to Manchester from Halifax at the age of seventeen. Crossley was keenly interested in literature too, was an omnivorous reader, and was already contributing to *Blackwood's Magazine*, one of the most important journals of the period, and to other literary reviews as well. William Harrison Ainsworth began to write seriously himself and clearly regarded a future as an author as preferable to one as a lawyer. Even before leaving

8. The man who invented the modern Dick Turpin: William Harrison Ainsworth at the age of thirty-four, from a portrait by J. R. Lane dating from 1839 (University of York Library).

9. Dick Turpin hiding in his cave in Epping Forest, from Richard Bayes's The Genuine History of the Life of Richard Turpin of 1739. Although there is no reason to suppose that this is an accurate depiction of Turpin, this is noteworthy as being the first visual image we have of him (Author's Collection).

school he wrote plays, which were staged in the cellar of his parents' house in King Street, and began himself to try to place work with the reviews (his first publication, a playlet published in *The Pocket Magazine*, came in 1821). But Ainsworth was no bookish recluse: he was a gregarious, personable and agreeable young man who began to make an impact on the Manchester social scene, being especially welcomed by the daughters of the city's elite. He and his friends would frequently meet at the Unicorn, an inn run by a widow Fisher. The young trainee solicitor was not immune from the heavy drinking that characterised the period; on one occasion Ainsworth and another friend, James Partingdon Aston, at one sitting drank three bottles of port and a bottle of claret between them.

At the age of nineteen William Harrison Ainsworth was, therefore, doing well. He had been born into a prosperous and stable family; he had good looks and an attractive personality; his duties in his father's firm were not over-onerous and left him with ample time to pursue his literary and social pursuits; while with James Crossley he was in the early stages of what was to prove to be a close and lifelong friendship. Then, in 1824, Harrison's father died, suddenly and prematurely at the age of forty-six, and the young and not very dedicated tyro lawyer found himself to be heir to the senior partnership in the firm of Ainsworth, Crossley and Sudlow. This was clearly beyond him, and he was sent to London to complete his legal training under the instruction of a barrister named Jacob Philips.

At first Ainsworth was full of good intentions. But if Manchester society offered pressing distractions that led him away from the law, London society offered infinitely more. He began to mix in literary and theatrical circles, carried on writing, and in 1826 authored, or perhaps more accurately co-authored, a novel entitled *Sir John Chiverton*. In that same year, his already uncertain interest in the law waned rapidly after he made the acquaintance of John Ebers, a publisher and owner of a circulating library who was also lessee of the Opera House in the Haymarket. Ainsworth established visiting terms with Ebers, and fell in love with his younger daughter, Fanny, regarded as one of the most beautiful girls in London society. The feeling was reciprocated, and in October 1826 the couple were married, both aged twenty-one. Ebers, apart from publishing several of Ainsworth's early works, set him up as a publisher and manager of his circulating library business, and the young couple initially lived with him at his home in Sussex Place in London, later taking a house a few doors away. Three daughters were born to the couple: Fanny in 1827, Emily in 1829, and Anne Blanche in 1830. The Ainsworths, young and attractive, living in one of the most fashionable streets in London, and connected as they were through John Ebers to the capital's literary world, entered London society in a big way. Ainsworth in particular enjoyed a semi-Bohemian existence of good dinners, ample wine, and the company of littérateurs and actresses, developing expensive tastes that were stay with him for the rest of his life.

All of this cost a great deal, and the Ainsworths' gilded existence was badly shaken when John Ebers' financial affairs crashed. They had to move to a less grand house, and Ainsworth had to find some means of earning money, which he did by opening his own law firm early in 1830. But once more, Ainsworth's taste for the literary world overcame such loyalty to the legal profession as he had, while he continued to demonstrate his talent for spending money, making an extensive continental tour in the summer of 1830. He did not give up writing, and was a founder member of one of the major journals of the period, *Fraser's Review*. Even so, it is difficult not to agree with Ainsworth's Edwardian biographer, that 'the year 1831 found Ainsworth twenty-six and, so far, not much of a success in life'. But it was that year which was to see the first steps towards Ainsworth's writing a novel entitled *Rookwood*, a book that was to transform the fortunes of William Harrison Ainsworth. It would also, and on a more permanent basis, transform those of the long-dead Dick Turpin.

There were two main influences at work on Ainsworth when he set about planning *Rookwood*. The first of these was the Gothic novel. This literary form, immensely popular between 1790 and 1820, owed its origins to Horace Walpole's *Castle of Otranto* of 1764, the second edition of which, published in the following year, was, in fact, subtitled *A Gothic Story*. 'Gothic' in this sense signified 'medieval', and hence 'barbarous', although the term came to be applied loosely to any period preceding the Enlightenment. Certainly, the Gothic novels that came into vogue from 1790 were usually set in the sixteenth and seventeenth centuries, and in the Catholic countries of southern Europe, which allowed for both exotic settings and anti-Catholic sentiments through the regular employment of hypocritical or malevolent nuns or monks as characters. The most important, most copied and probably most highly paid of these Gothic novelists was Ann Radcliffe, for whom Ainsworth was to admit his admiration. Radcliffe, daughter of a London tradesman and wife of another lawyer with literary ambitions, published *The Romance of the Forest*, which appeared in 1791. Her most successful novel, *The Mysteries of Udolpho*, appeared in

1794. It established one of the stereotypical characters of the genre, the female heroine who found herself trapped in a sinister building by an aristocratic villain. Radcliffe's books and those of her imitators and successors were characterised by mysterious castles or monasteries with an excess of secret passages and dungeons, by vivid descriptions of landscape and climatic conditions, by the tyranny of wicked fathers and uncles over abducted or orphaned daughters and nieces, and by plots that were wild and implausible but full of suspense and incident.

The second main influence on *Rookwood* was a relatively new genre that was replacing the Gothic as the most fashionable novel form, the historical novel. This genre was associated with one of the great literary figures of the early nineteenth century, Sir Walter Scott. Born in Edinburgh in 1771 and, like Ainsworth, destined for a legal career, Scott was another young lawyer who preferred literary fame. He too wrote extensively for the reviews, although his first major successes were poetic works, notably *The Lay of the Last Minstrel* in 1805 and *Marmion* in 1808. His literary career really took off, however, in 1814 (by which point he had also experienced considerable success in the law) with the publication of an historical novel, *Waverley*: five other novels inspired by Scottish historical themes followed by 1818. The following year, 1819, was to witness the publication of his greatest success, *Ivanhoe*. By this time (he was to die in 1832) Scott was phenomenally successful commercially, and also enjoyed an incalculable influence as a novelist. Ainsworth, for example, was to take considerable pride in the praise Scott gave to his novel of 1826, *Sir John Chiverton*.

It was thus the Gothic novels of Ann Radcliffe, and the historical novel as created by Sir Walter Scott, that were

Ainsworth's major influences when he set about the composition of *Rookwood*. He had resolved 'to attempt a story in the
bygone style of Mrs Radcliffe (which had always inexpressible
charms for me), substituting an old English squire, and old
English manorial residence, and an old English highwayman
for the Italian marchese, the castle, and the brigand of the great
mistress of romance'. While walking through the cemetery of
Chesterfield Church (a building then, as now, distinguished by
its leaning steeple), he witnessed the opening of a vault, which
gave him the idea for the first scene of his projected novel. He
had to let the project rest for two years, as he was heavily
involved in trying to clear up his father-in-law's financial affairs.
But in 1833 he was able to resume work on *Rookwood*, being
inspired especially by a stay at Cuckfield Place in Sussex, an old
house of Elizabethan origins that formed the prototype for the
Rookwood Place of the novel. Thus *Rookwood* fell together
almost haphazardly over a period of several years, and it is
unclear if Ainsworth at any point thought through a coherent
plot for it; the book gives the impression of having been constructed by fits and starts, with the narrative threads being pulled
together when opportunity allowed. Nevertheless, Ainsworth
managed to place the work with Richard Bentley, one of the
most successful publishers of the day, and it appeared, in three
volumes, in April 1834.

To the modern reader, *Rookwood* is a very curious literary production. Its plot is almost impossible to summarise, dependent

as it is on rapidly changing action and on those dramatic episodes essential to works that were published in a period when the dominant serial form accustomed readers to frequent cliff-hanging incidents. Briefly, the story, set in 1737, concerns the fortunes of the Rookwood family of Rookwood Place in West Yorkshire. It opens a few days after the death of the head of the family, Sir Piers Rookwood, and its central theme is the disputed succession between Sir Piers's son Ranulph and Luke Rookwood, who is known publicly as Sir Piers's illegitimate son, but who is, in reality, the fruit of a secret marriage between Sir Piers and Susan Bradley. Susan had died soon after the birth of Luke, being in fact murdered by Father Checkley, the Jesuit priest who had married the couple. Later in the story, however, it is discovered that Sir Piers has in fact willed the family estate to his great-niece, Eleanor Mowbray. Ranulph has already met Eleanor, and has fallen in love with her, but, on discovering that she is to inherit the estate, Luke decides to marry her against her will. He is already betrothed to a gipsy, Sybil, granddaughter to Barbara, the queen of a tribe of gipsies who live in a ruined abbey nearby. Sybil, delegated to murder Eleanor by her grandmother, prefers to commit suicide, and the marriage between Luke and Eleanor goes forward, with the bride drugged and insensible. But Barbara sends Luke a lock of the dead Sybil's hair, which is poisoned and kills him instantly when he touches it. This leaves the way clear for Ranulph and Eleanor to marry (she is, by now, reciprocating his affections), and thus all ends happily.

Gothic elements loom large in the novel. There was a family custom of male Rookwoods murdering their wives, while more generally the death of a member of the family was invariably presaged by a branch falling off the 'Doom Tree', which stood just outside Rookwood Place. But perhaps the most truly Gothic element in the book was the setting of two of the key scenes in the family vault of the Rookwoods. The novel opens in the vault, at midnight, with Luke Rookwood and Peter Bradley, the sexton, sitting on a coffin and discussing the death of Sir Piers over a bottle of spirits. It is at this point that the sexton reveals to Luke that he is, in fact, Sir Piers's legitimate heir, and in his surprise the young man accidentally dislodges a pile of coffins, one of which splits open to reveal his long-dead mother, embalmed and still perfectly preserved. Peter Bradley, it transpires in another of the plot's many twists, is, indeed, Alan Rookwood, uncle to Sir Piers, who was believed to have died many years previously, and he is to meet his end in the vault, along with Sir Piers's widow, the fairly dreadful Maud, daughter of Sir Thomas D'Aubeny. The former sexton waits in the vault for the arrival of Luke, who had already been poisoned by the lock of Sybil's hair, when Lady Maud enters. She (to the modern reader perhaps understandably in the light of recent events in her family) has become deranged, and has followed what she believed to be Sir Piers's ghost into the vault. She claims that the spectre was pointing at a particular sarcophagus, and Alan, at her request, manages to open it. The sarcophagus contains the remains of the first of the Rookwoods, Sir Ranulph, and the dagger with which he had initiated the family custom of wife-killing. Moved by this discovery, Lady Maud enters the sarcophagus and attempts to take the dagger, at which point Alan, who is holding the heavy lid of the tomb open, discovers there is a mechanism to deter those trying to open the monument, a crucial element in which is an axe that is about to strike his head. In his alarm he drops the lid of the sarcophagus, trapping Lady Maud inside, and is unable to reopen it ('she uttered one shriek, and the lid closed for ever'). But on entering the vault Maud had inadvertently locked the vault door (the key was on the outside) that Alan had left ajar for Luke, and so he too was trapped. He died after three days' confinement, his final act being to find the coffin of his hated brother, Reginald, and utter a curse on him with his last breath.

The main story-line of *Rookwood* is essentially a plot without a hero: Luke, the central character, is too gloomy and too ill fated, while his half-brother Ranulph is poorly delineated and does not play a very strong role in the narrative. The book's most memorable character is the main figure in the sub-plot, Dick Turpin. The highwayman first appears as 'Jack Palmer', a hearty sort of fellow who is obviously meant to be a romanticised version of that John Palmer who mixed with the local gentry in East Yorkshire and Lincolnshire in the late 1730s: 'Who he was, or whence he came, was a question not easily answered – Jack, himself, evading all solution to the inquiry ... nobody ... knew anything about him, save that he was a capital judge of horseflesh, kept a famous black mare, and attended every hunt in the West Riding – that he could sing a good song, was a choice companion, and could drink three bottles without feeling the worse for them.'

In due course Ainsworth reveals Jack Palmer to be Dick Turpin the Highwayman, a character who is depicted in tones of flowery approbation by Ainsworth:

Rash daring was the main feature of Turpin's character. Like our great Nelson, he knew fear only by name ... possessed of the belief that his hour was not yet come, he cared little or nothing for any risk he might incur; and though he might, undoubtedly, have some presentiment of the probable termination of his career, he never suffered it to militate against his present enjoyment, which proved that he was no despicable philosopher. Turpin was the *ultimus Romanorum*, the last of a race, which (we were almost about to say we regret) is now altogether extinct. Several successors he had, it is true, but no name worthy to be recorded after his own. With him expired the chivalrous spirit which animated so many knights of the road; with him died away that passionate love of enterprise, that high spirit of devotion to the fair sex ...

And if Ainsworth romanticised Turpin, he did much the same for the highwayman in general. Shortly after his first appearance in the novel, we find Jack Palmer discussing highwaymen with the Irish doctor Titus Tyrconnel and the lawyer Codicil Coates, who, as the story unfolds, is to become Turpin's implacable enemy. Coates questions the premise that a highwayman can be a gentleman, a proposition which Turpin, *alias* Palmer, defends roundly:

I don't see how it can be otherwise. It is as necessary for a man to be a gentleman before he can turn highwayman, as it is for a doctor to have his diploma, or an attorney his certificate. Some of the finest gentlemen of their days, as captains Lovelace, Hind, Hannum, and Dudley, were eminent on the road and they set the fashion. Ever since their day a real highwayman would consider himself disgraced, if he did not conduct himself in every way like a gentleman.

Later in the same speech, Turpin declares that 'England, Sir, has reason to be proud of her highwaymen! They are peculiar to her clime, and are as much before the brigand of Italy, the contrabandist of Spain, or the cut-purse of France — as her sailors are before all the rest of the world.' The highwayman, apparently, could now be regarded by patriots as a source of national pride.

Thus in *Rookwood* Ainsworth not only created a fictionalised image of Dick Turpin, but also re-created the highwayman as an heroic figure, a gentleman of the road, courageous, brave, an embodiment of English virtues as perceived in the 1830s, an entity whose passing was to be regretted. Our idea of Turpin as a romantic hero, and our broader romantic notions about highwaymen, owe almost everything to *Rookwood*.

Ainsworth's novel made two specific contributions of tremendous importance to the Turpin legend: it provided him with his faithful steed, Black Bess, and also attached his name firmly to the ride to York. Ainsworth wrote the passages dealing with the ride to York in a remarkable bout of sustained composition. His own account records his writing methods, and also illustrates his style. He was, at the time of writing, living at a house called The Elms in Kilburn, and simply sat down and composed the hundred or so pages describing Turpin's ride to York in one 24-hour sitting:

Well do I remember the fever into which I was thrown during the time of composition. My pen literally scoured over the pages. So thoroughly did I identify with the highwayman, that, once I started, I found it impossible to halt. Animated by kindred enthusiasm, I cleared every obstacle in my path with as much facility as Turpin disposed of the impediments that beset his flight. In his company I mounted the hill-side, dashed through the bustling village, swept over the desolate heath, threaded the silent street, plunged into the eddying stream, and kept an onward course, without pause, without hindrance, without fatigue. With him I shouted, sang, laughed, exulted, wept. Nor did I retire to rest till, in imagination, I heard the bell of York Minster toll forth the death of poor Black Bess.

Ainsworth also, to his credit, checked the route before publication, to ensure that his topographical details were accurate. But his description of how the account of the ride was written, routinely published as part of the preface to later editions of *Rookwood*, catches the spirit of Book IV of the novel. This consists entirely of the account of how Dick Turpin and Black Bess, overcoming fatigue and all opposition, rode from London to York between evening and morning, and how Bess died within sight of York Minster.

Book IV of *Rookwood* opens with Turpin and three associates meeting at an inn at Kilburn, a place that was, as Ainsworth explains to his readers, in 1737 little more than a hamlet. The most important of these associates is Tom King, a languidly handsome young highwayman, in Ainsworth's words 'a noted high-tobygloak of his time, who obtained, from his appearance and address, the sobriquet of the "Gentleman Highwayman"'. The other two present were a pair of characters who had already been introduced at the gipsy camp in Yorkshire, Jerry Juniper and Zoroaster. Turpin had carried out a robbery on his adversary, the lawyer Coates, and was also anxious about how Luke Rookwood was faring, and so had made his mind up to return to Yorkshire. But while the four criminals were drinking and singing, a posse headed by Coates and the chief constable of Middlesex were gathering around the inn, for Turpin and King had been betrayed by one of King's women friends. The two highwaymen were caught in the very act of mounting their horses, and, although Turpin broke free, King was taken by the chief constable. Turpin returned, and on King's insistence tried to shoot the constable. His first shot went through the sleeve of the officer's coat, but the second struck King in the chest, wounding him fatally, this whole episode being clearly a reworking of the events that had led to the real-life shooting of Matthew King. In the novel, Tom King died more or less instantly, but not before learning of his betrayal. Turpin made his escape, and decided to evade the posse by riding to York: 'His bosom throbbed high with rapture', Ainsworth wrote, 'and he involuntarily exclaimed aloud, as he raised himself in the saddle, "By God! I will do it!"'

This is the beginning of the most famous equestrian feat in English literature and English legend. Constantly pursued by a party whose resolve was hardened by the hatred Coates harboured for Turpin, a party that was also able to benefit from regular changes of horses, Turpin and Black Bess set out on their journey, making their way through the lanes and country roads to the north of Kilburn, jumping the tollgate at Hornsey, running the gauntlet of 'the long straggling town of Tottenham', riding through Edmonton to cries of approbation from the townsfolk, and then headed north, passing through Huntingdon, Stamford, Grantham and up into Yorkshire. The journey was, needless to say, packed with incident, perhaps the most memorable being Turpin's stopping at an inn to revive a flagging Black Bess by rubbing her down with a solution of water and brandy, and by rubbing the bit of her bridle with raw beefsteak. There are many passages that express the thrill of the ride, a typical one beginning with Turpin's exhilaration:

> His blood spins through his veins; winds round his heart; mounts to his brain. Away! Away! He is wild with joy. Hall, cot, tree, tower, glade, mead, waste, or woodland are seen, passed, left behind, and vanish as in a dream. Motion is scarcely perceptible – it is impetus! Volition! the horse and her rider are driven forward, as it were, by self-accelerated speed. A hamlet is visible in the moonlight. It is scarcely discovered ere the flints sparkle beneath the mare's hoofs. A moment's clatter upon the stones, and it is left behind. Again, it is the silent, smiling country. Now they are buried in the darkness of woods; now sweeping along on the wide plain; now clearing the unopened toll-bar; now trampling over the hollow-sounding bridge, their shadows momentarily reflected in the placid mirror of the stream; now scaling the hill-side a thought more slowly; now plunging, as the horses of Phoebus into the ocean, down its precipitous sides.

But the pursuit is never far behind them, and at Cawood, about ten miles outside York, Dick has to swim Bess across the Ouse to avoid capture, and, with the posse still close behind, rides down on to what is now the A19 and is set to enter York via Fulford.

Black Bess was, as Ainsworth put it, 'undoubtedly the heroine of the Fourth Book of this Romance'. The mare was born of a desert Arabian, 'brought to this country by a wealthy traveller', and an English racer, 'coal-black as her child'. 'In colour she was perfectly black, with a skin smooth on the surface as polished jet; not a single white hair could be detected in her satin coat.' The eulogy continued: 'In make she was magnificent, every point was perfect, beautiful, compact'; 'look at her elegant little head'; 'she was built more for strength than beauty, and yet she *was* beautiful'; 'as to her temper, the lamb is not more gentle. A child might guide her.' Ainsworth's description of Bess has earned her a special place in the pantheon of great animals in literature. 'And thou, too, brave Bess', Ainsworth has Turpin say as he contemplates how the ride to York will earn him immortality, 'thy name shall be linked with mine, and we'll go down to posterity together.' This was a remarkably accurate prophecy.

Yet Bess was not to survive the ride to York. Beyond Fulford, about a mile from the centre of York, the mare finally collapsed: 'Bess tottered – fell. There was a dreadful gasp – a parting moan – a snort; her eye gazed, for an instant, upon her master, with a dying glare; then grew glassy, rayless, fixed. A shiver ran through her frame. Her heart had burst.' Turpin stands distraught by her body, only to be roused from his depression by the sound of the bells of York Minster striking 6 a.m., and by a slap on his shoulder delivered by another of his gipsy associates, Balthazar, who is conveniently in the area and, even more conveniently, carrying a pack with a change of clothing in it. This is given to Turpin, who makes off, and Balthazar then fields the pursuers who arrive shortly afterwards. After some questioning, they conclude that Turpin has escaped, leave the body of Bess in Balthazar's keeping, and head off to the Bowling-Green Inn for breakfast. As they await the arrival of their food, they fall into conversation with a countryman in a smock-frock who was eating breakfast near them, 'an odd-looking fellow, with a terrible squint, and a strange contorted countenance'. The rustic was, of course, that master of disguise, Dick Turpin.

Whilst admiring Ainsworth's capacity for telling the story, it is worth pondering where the connection between Turpin and the ride to York, and his ownership of a mare named Black Bess, came from. A probable solution to this first problem has been suggested by Derek Barlow, that indefatigable researcher into Turpin sources. Barlow discovered a rare copy of a tract, published in 1808, which gave a very brief narrative of Turpin's ride to York, based on Defoe's earlier account of the exploit of 'Swift Nicks', with the added suggestion, developed by Ainsworth, that Turpin rode with raw beef on his horse's bit. It is highly likely that Ainsworth was familiar with this pamphlet, and drew on it when creating the idea of Turpin's ride to York as a central episode in *Rookwood*. At the very least, the existence of this pamphlet (and it might have been just one of a number of ephemeral works about Turpin that were then in circulation and have since been lost) demonstrates that Ainsworth cannot be credited with inventing the notion that it was Turpin who rode to York.

A clue to the origins of Black Bess is provided by Horace Smith's *Gaieties and Gravities*, published in 1825. This contains a story called 'Harry Halter', in which appears a ballad entitled 'Turpin and the Bishop' which begins with the lines 'Bold Turpin upon Hounslow Heath/ His black mare Bess bestrode'. The 'black mare Bess' was, in a stroke of alliterative genius, changed to 'Black Bess' by Ainsworth. One wonders, however, how many references to black mares named Bess there were in stories of eighteenth-century highwaymen, while it is possible that Ainsworth may have been led to his felicitous rejigging of 'the black mare Bess' by a country dance called 'Black Bess', with which he might have been familiar in his youth.

So Ainsworth was responsible neither for originally ascribing the ride to York to Turpin, nor for originating the idea that Turpin rode a black mare called Bess. Yet this should not detract from Ainsworth's achievement. For it is undeniable that whatever references Ainsworth was drawing on, it was the phenomenal success of *Rookwood* that firmly established those two crucial elements of the Turpin legend: that Dick Turpin was the highwayman who made the epic ride from London to York, and that he did so upon a faithful mare named Black Bess.

This in turn began the modern myth of the highwayman as a gentlemanly daredevil hero. And in this last point there is a certain irony. *Rookwood* was published in April 1834. The last old-style mounted highway robbery, as a parliamentary commission on the implementation of county police forces reported in 1839, had occurred near Taunton in 1831, and had been followed by the execution of the robber. The commissioners, while decrying the number of robberies carried out by footpads, could find 'no traces of mounted highway robbers amongst the class of habitual depredators', and were also unable to find 'recent cases of the robbery of mails, or of travellers in stage coaches by robbers of that description'. The report ascribed the 'suppression of highway robberies in the vicinity of the metropolis' to the introduction of patrols of armed mounted police, and noted that highway robberies on the fringes of provincial towns had been 'rendered more hazardous than heretofore by the increased number of turnpikes and other means of recognition and detection'. Other changes helped too. The development of banking and credit facilities meant that travellers were increasingly unlikely to have to carry large sums of money, urban growth had planted houses on the highwayman's old haunts, while over the next two decades the development of a railway system was to make the stage-coach and even the lengthy horse-journey things of the past. Consciously or otherwise, Ainsworth invested Dick Turpin and the English highwayman with heroic qualities at exactly the point when the reality of highway robbery, in its classic form, had ceased to be a threat.

Rookwood was an instant success. 'His story is one that never flags ... we expect much from this writer', declared the *Quarterly Review*. The reviewer in *The Spectator* thought the work to have been written 'with great vigour and wonderful variety'. 'It is long since such a work as this has been produced – the author exhibits ability of no ordinary kind', *The Atlas* informed its readers. In a letter to the young publisher John Macrone, Ainsworth also mentioned favourable reviews in a number of other journals. The book was a massively popular as well as a critical success. The first printing rapidly sold out, and it was published again in August 1834. A third edition was published in 1835 by Macrone, who was also to publish the fourth edition a year later. This last added another dimension to the growing Turpin legend by being illustrated with engravings by George Cruikshank, bringing another major figure of the mid nineteenth century into the story. A fifth edition, the sixtieth volume in Bentley's Standard Novel Series, was to follow in 1837.

Thereafter the work was to be reprinted regularly by a variety of publishers well into the twentieth century. A French translation, appropriately entitled *Les Gentilshommes de Grand Chemin*, was published in Paris in 1836, and a German translation at Leipzig a year later, while the book was also translated into Dutch at an early stage. There can be no doubt that *Rookwood* had a formidable impact. As its publishing history shows, it sold remarkably well, and was one of the most successful novels of the nineteenth century. It was much discussed by the reading public of the day and it created, via dramatisations, series of prints of incidents on the ride to York and other means, a remarkable vogue for Dick Turpin. Its author rocketed from obscurity to celebrity. He became the literary lion of 1834, and proof of the extent of the fame that the publication of *Rookwood* brought him came when his portrait decorated the horse-drawn omnibuses that had been introduced in London a few years earlier.

Ainsworth was now faced with the problem of following this remarkable success. His next novel, *Crichton*, after various delays, was published in three volumes in February 1837. Set in sixteenth-century France and involving the adventures of a young Scotsman at the court of Henri III, this was a more straightforwardly historical novel in the Sir Walter Scott mode, and, despite its qualities as an example of that genre, it failed to strike as strong a responsive chord among the reading public as had *Rookwood*, although it too was dramatised on the London stage, and was translated into a number of languages. Perhaps disappointed by the relatively cool reception afforded to *Crichton*, Ainsworth returned to eighteenth-century criminals for the theme for his next novel, *Jack Sheppard*, another character whom the author claimed to have remembered from his boyhood reading.

Jack Sheppard first appeared in serial form in *Bentley's Miscellany* (Richard Bentley was the publisher with whom Ainsworth was working at this stage). Starting in the January 1839 issue, and concluding in February 1840, it proved a massive success. It was published as a three-volume novel before the end of its serialisation, in October 1839, embellished with twenty-seven engravings by Cruikshank and a portrait of Ainsworth. The career of the historical Jack Sheppard, exciting enough in itself, was reworked to provide the necessary elements of shock and melodrama, while the novel contained numerous other characters adapted from criminal history and legend, among them the man who was to cause Jack's downfall, the criminal entrepreneur Jonathan Wild. The novel was a success on a par with *Rookwood*, outselling Charles Dickens's *Oliver Twist*, which was published at about the same time. It was dramatised – eight different plays on the theme of Sheppard appearing in the autumn of 1839 – and spawned numerous imitative works in the form of lives and memoirs of Sheppard that appeared in large numbers in the years following its publication. Despite adverse comment on the effect on public morals of glorifying the life of a criminal and, by extension, crime in general, Sheppard as reinvented by Ainsworth proved, in the medium term, to be as successful a fictional character as his own reinvented Dick Turpin. And the success of the novel firmly reinstated Ainsworth as one of the leading novelists of his day.

Ainsworth's newly acquired prestige meant he was invited to two of the leading salons in London, those of Lady Marguerite Blessington and Lord and Lady Holland, both of them frequented by the rich, famous and powerful. And there can be no doubt of Ainsworth's suitability as a member of the *beau monde*. Not only was he successful, personable and witty, but he was also, by all accounts, extremely handsome. A friend remembered him at the time of his first successes as

> a handsome man, but it was very much of the barber's block type of beauty, with wavy scented hair, smiling lips, and a pink and white complexion. As a young man he was gorgeous in the *outré* dress of the dandy of '36, and in common with those famous dandies D'Orsay, young Benjamin Disraeli, and Tom Duncombe, wore multitudinous waistcoats, over which dangled a long gold chain, and numerous rings.

So success brought celebrity and a wide social acceptance to Ainsworth. It also wrecked his marriage. Early in 1835 Fanny left Ainsworth and went to live with her father. The exact circumstances of the collapse of the marriage remain unclear. S. M. Ellis, the main source for Ainsworth's life, simply referred to the marriage becoming 'clouded with differences', and claimed that even when he wrote, in 1911, it was impossible to reconstruct what happened. Ellis, however, is weak on Ainsworth's domestic life, and Fanny figures very little in his account of Ainsworth's activities between the marriage in 1826 and its dissolution. Ellis says simply that Fanny 'did not participate in the fame and pleasures which accrued from the literary success of her husband', although Ainsworth had more or less led an independent social life for some time before *Rookwood* made him famous. When success was added to his good looks, he must have been extremely attractive to members of the opposite sex, and the 'differences' to which Ellis refers might have arisen from infidelity on Ainsworth's part. Perhaps significantly, the commentary that accompanied a sketch of Ainsworth which appeared in the July 1834 edition of *Fraser's Magazine* makes some clear allusions:

> We have not had the pleasure of being acquainted with Mrs
> Ainsworth, but we are sincerely sorry for her – we deeply com-
> miserate her case. You see what a pretty fellow THE young nov-
> elist of the season is; how exactly, in fact, he resembles one of the
> most classically handsome and brilliant of the established lady
> killers ... alas! It were well if 'balls assemblies and plays' were
> all, there are also such things, not un-dreamt of in the philoso-
> phy of the Mayfair fair ones, as *boudoirs* and *tête-à-têtes*; and the
> best we can say for this Turpin of the cabriolet, whose prancer
> will never masticate a beefsteak, is, that if he ever escapes scot-
> free during the first month of the blaze of his romance, he is a
> lucky as well as a well-grown lad.

One suspects that Ainsworth fell all too readily into the tempta-
tions so strongly hinted at here, with disastrous consequences for
his marriage. Fanny was to die in March 1838, at the age of
thirty-three.

Ainsworth set up house with what Ellis refers to as his 'connections', Mrs James Touchet and her sister Miss Buckley, at
Kensal Lodge on the Harrow Road, later moving, at the height
of his fame, to the adjacent Kensal Manor House. At that time
Kensal Lodge and Kensal Manor House were two of three
buildings which stood quite alone on the road between the ham-
lets of Kensal Green and Harlsden Green, in an attractive rural
district. For fourteen years these two buildings successively
became leading centres of London literary life. Now famous,

Ainsworth became a lavish entertainer, and made his home an important rendezvous for early Victorian writers and their associates. Many of those who came to dine at Kensal Lodge or Kensal Manor House – although, like Ainsworth, important figures in their day – are now forgotten. But among them were Thackeray, George Cruikshank the artist, illustrator of some of Dickens's work as well as some of Ainsworth's, and extremely good company before he turned teetotal; Benjamin Disraeli, in the 1830s a fashionable young man about town; and, above all, Charles Dickens. This last was an unknown journalist aged twenty-two when Ainsworth took him under his wing, and the successful author did much to encourage the younger man and aid the early stages of his career. The two novelists, despite their professional rivalry, were to remain good friends well into the 1850s.

Although Ainsworth was to write prolifically for nearly another forty years, his fortunes began to decline from about 1842 onwards. He spent considerable time on the editorship of magazines, having founded his own, *Ainsworth's Magazine*, in February 1842 (he was to close it in 1854, evidence of his waning popularity), and perhaps he devoted too much of his energies to editorship, a task that he took extremely seriously. More importantly, the tastes of the reading public were changing, and the type of novel in which Ainsworth specialised was no longer fashionable. The public now wanted novels based on contemporary or near-contemporary themes, with a prevailing tone of domestic realism rather than Gothic horrors or historical narratives. This was a style best deployed by Charles Dickens and Thackeray, who had replaced Ainsworth as Britain's best-selling novelists, and which was to be carried further within a

George Cruickshank

10. *The death of Black Bess at the end of the ride to York, one of George Cruickshank's illustrations for Ainsworth's* Rookwood *which first appeared in the third edition of 1835. Note that the modern image of Turpin had yet to be finalized (© Dean and Chapter of York: By kind permission).*

few years by Anthony Trollope and George Eliot. There were still some successes to come, notably *The Lancashire Witches*, which was published in serial form in *The Sunday Times* in 1848 and as a novel in the subsequent year: but Ainsworth's status as a literary lion had gone.

The situation was compounded by the fact that Ainsworth was a poor manager of his finances. Although the money came in rapidly in the years of his greatest success, it disappeared just as quickly, poured out by Ainsworth, the lavish entertainer, the performer of countless acts of generosity, the bon viveur, the lover of lengthy continental holidays. In 1853 he had to give up Kensal Manor House, and the literary and artistic gatherings ceased. In the first of a series of moves, always to smaller houses, he went to Brighton, where he still entertained regularly, and where a number of his old London literary friends visited. But his fortunes continued to decline, and he moved to Tunbridge Wells in 1867, and then to a variety of other locations, eventually making his last move, to Reigate, in 1878. Although he was still writing a novel a year throughout the 1860s, his unfashionability meant that the money he earned declined massively. In 1848 the *Sunday Times* had paid him £1,000 for *The Lancashire Witches*: in 1874 he was to get a mere £150 for *The Lancashire Rebels and the Fatal '45*. The family property had to be sold off. The home on King Street, Manchester, where Ainsworth had been born, was sold in 1860, and in 1864 Beech Hill, the house just outside Manchester where Ainsworth had enjoyed such happy boyhood summers, followed. In 1878 the last item of his patrimony, the old Ainsworth house at Spotland Gate, had to be sold as well.

By then Ainsworth had long lost touch with the literary

circle of which he had been such an important member in the
1840s. Percy Fitzgerald, author of a biography of Dickens,
remembered a literary dinner in the 1860s given by the publisher
Frederic Chapman, at which John Forster, a former friend of
Ainsworth and Dickens, and Robert Browning were present.
Fitzgerald recalled how Browning said humorously, 'A sad, for-
lorn looking being stopped me today, and reminded me of old
times. He presently resolved himself into – whom do you think?
– Harrison Ainsworth!' Forster responded, 'Good Heavens! Is
he still alive?' Ainsworth was indeed alive, was still writing
books, and, ironically, was to outlive both Browning and
Forster. But his existence was by now more or less marginal to
that London literary society to which he had so avidly aspired
and by which he had once been so fêted.

Yet he was to have one final moment of glory. On Thursday
15 September 1881 Ainsworth was the guest at a dinner given
in his honour by the mayor of Manchester. Whatever the
decline of his reputation in metropolitan circles, the geographical location of the plots of a number of his later novels had
given him the nickname of 'The Lancashire Novelist', and
Manchester was obviously determined to provide lavish, if
somewhat belated, honours for one of its more notable sons. At
the dinner, which, happily, was attended by Ainsworth's old
friend Crossley, the mayor gave a speech in which he not only
praised the author, but also gave some statistical evidence of his
enduring popularity among what he described as 'the artisan
class of readers'. He told how there were 250 volumes of
Ainsworth's works in the Manchester free libraries, and that
during the previous months these had been borrowed 7,660
times, so that, on average, twenty of Ainsworth's books were

taken out to be read on any one day. The most popular of these was *The Tower of London*, followed by *The Lancashire Witches* and *Old St Paul's* (interestingly, *Rookwood* neither figured among the three of Ainsworth's novels most read in Manchester, nor among three other works cited by the mayor as being especially frequently read). Ainsworth gave a speech that demonstrated, if the account of it is accurate, that he had lost none of his mental powers nor his ability to charm.

He died four months later. In his final surviving letter, written to his friend Dr James Bower on 28 December 1881, he mentioned that he had been troubled by the foggy weather of the previous week, and that his doctor 'thought me much wasted since I last saw him'. Five days later, on 3 January 1882, he died of congestion on the lungs. He was buried, as was his wish, in the vault in Kensal Green cemetery where his mother and brother were already interred, his body on the day of the burial taking a last trip down the Harrow Road along which so many visitors had come to his house in the 1840s. He had married again in the 1860s, to a Sarah Wells (a daughter, Clara, had been born in 1867, when Ainsworth was aged sixty-two), and his widow attended the funeral, along with his daughters Fanny and Anne Blanche (the only one of his three daughters by Fanny Ebers to marry), his publishers, and about a dozen other relatives and friends. His great friend James Crossley was too aged to travel from Manchester to the funeral, and was himself to die within a year.

This was the quiet end of William Harrison Ainsworth, one of the most celebrated authors of his day, writer of some forty novels and innumerable essays and reviews, the man whose third novel outsold *Oliver Twist*, the friend and early patron of

Charles Dickens and William Makepeace Thackeray, the generous host and the loyal friend. His books were popular well into the twentieth century, although they are now virtually unread, and their author, once such a literary lion, is now largely unknown. Conversely, Ainsworth's greatest literary creation lives on. Dick Turpin, the man whom Ainsworth did so much to reinvent, and whose character he so thoroughly refurbished, remains as familiar and as celebrated as ever. If for nothing else, Ainsworth deserves his place in the cultural history of England for inventing one of those very few historical figures whom all of us recognise. For it is essentially Ainsworth's Turpin that we remember and celebrate today, not the pockmarked man who swung from the 'Three-Legged Mare' at York in 1739.

chapter *six*

TURPIN HERO

In 1869 the journalist and writer James Greenwood published *The Seven Curses of London*, a work that was to achieve the status of a major exposé of the mid-Victorian metropolitan underclass. Among the locations he visited while researching his book was what he described as 'a prison in the suburbs of London, one of the largest, and as far as I have opportunity of judging, one of the best managed and conducted'. The governor of this institution, for Greenwood's benefit, interviewed a youthful criminal ('a very bad lad') who had recently been admitted to the prison for theft. Part of the interview, as recorded by Greenwood, ran as follows:

GOVERNOR. He only came in yesterday, and to-day, while out for exercise with the others, he must misconduct himself, and when the warder reproved him, he must swear some horrible oath against him. It is for that he is here. How many times have you been here, lad?

LAD [*gulping desperately*]. Three times, sir!

GOVERNOR [*sternly*]. What! Speak the truth, lad.

LAD [*with a determined effort to gouge tears of his eyes with his knuckles*]. Four times, sir.

GOVERNOR . Four times! And so you'll go on till you are sent away, I'm afraid. Can you read, lad?

LAD [*with a penitential wriggle*]. Yes, sir; I wish as I couldn't, sir.

GOVERNOR . Ah! Why so?

LAD [*with a doleful wag of his bullet head*]. Cos then I shouldn't have read none of them highwaymen's books, sir; it was them as was the beginning of it.

The young thief blamed the beginning of his slide into delinquency on reading 'them highwaymen's books' as a tactic aimed at ingratiating himself with authority. The prison governor (like Greenwood) regarded reading what we would today classify as pulp fiction as a major cause of crime among working-class youth. Whatever the truthfulness of the bullet-headed lad's claims, thanks to the success of William Harrison Ainsworth's *Rookwood* and the cognate notoriety of the newly launched and totally reinvented Dick Turpin, there was no shortage of 'highwaymen's books' around to be read at the time when the young thief described by Greenwood was forming his reading habits.

The success of *Rookwood* in 1834, and the immediate popularity of what came to be considered as that novel's central figure, Dick Turpin, initiated a massive vogue for the literature of highwaymen. Publications about highwaymen had appeared spasmodically over the earlier years of the nineteenth century, but the success of Ainsworth's novel and of his great fictional creation ensured that the highwayman became a central figure in popular literature for the next two or three generations. New editions of Johnson's *The Lives and Actions of the most famous Highwaymen* (with slight variations of title) were published in 1839, 1844 and around 1850 (the first at least containing no mention of Turpin), while new editions of another work that originated in the eighteenth century, *A genuine History of the Lives and Actions of the most notorious Irish Highwaymen, Tories, and Raparees*, appeared in 1839 and 1850. An edition of the *Newgate Calendar*, a compendium of short accounts of the lives of notorious highwaymen and other criminals, appeared around 1840. *The Lives of notorious and daring Highwaymen and Robbers, compiled from authentic Sources*, ascribed to a G. Thompson, but heavily dependent on the eighteenth-century works, appeared in 1843 and was reprinted in 1846, while Charles Whitehead's *Lives and Exploits of English Highwaymen, Pirates and Robbers* appeared in two volumes in 1834, obviously well timed to exploit the taste for such stories *Rookwood* had created. The demand remained undiminished throughout the nineteenth century as shown by such publications as *Tales of Highwaymen: or, the Romance of the Road*, which first appeared in serial form in 1865 and continued to be republished in the 1870s.

Individual highwaymen also attracted attention from hack authors. It is no surprise that the dashing Claude Duval, that prototype of the romantic highway robber, appears to have been an especially popular subject, with a number of post-*Rookwood* publications adding to Duval's long-running fame. E. C. Grey, one of the established popular writers of the period, published around 1850 his *Claude Duval, the Dashing Highwayman. A Tale of the Road*, and that year was to see an anonymous work, *The Life and Adventures of Claude Duval, the dashing Highwayman*, published in New York. *Nightshade: or Claude Duval, the dashing Highwayman*, followed in 1865. Four years later there came a 'burlesque-sensational drama', *Claude Du Val: or, the Highwayman for the Ladies*, a play of considerable dreadfulness, which at least has the virtue of reminding us that works produced for the popular theatre in the mid-Victorian period could be as dire as some of the worst offerings of modern television. *The Life of Jack Rann, alias sixteen-string Jack, the noted Highwayman*, another figure whose exploits were to form the basis for numerous Victorian publications, appeared in 1834. Tom King, Turpin's friend in *Rookwood* and another entirely fictional prototype of the dare-devil and gallant highwayman, had to wait until 1884 to have a novel devoted to him, entitled *Tom King, the Hero Highwayman, or, Stand and Deliver*. This work was followed a year later by an anonymous work, *Tom King the Dashing Highwayman*.

But, despite the popularity of these other figures, it was Turpin who was to be the most consistently successful fictional highwayman. His fame, already established by *Rookwood,* was cemented by Henry Downes Miles's novel *Dick Turpin*, first published in 1840. In his preface to the fourth edition, published in 1844, Miles informed his readers that his novel could demonstrate 'the best criterion of approval', having sold 20,000 copies. Miles was a prolific writer, whose other publications included a novel centred on Claude Duval, an Anglo-Indian phrase book, and a history of British boxing, and employed in his fiction a prose style that was even more embedded in the melodramatic mode of the period than Ainsworth's. Consider, for example, his depiction of the scene as Turpin, on the outskirts of York (which in Miles's account he approached via another route than that sketched by Ainsworth) witnesses the death of Black Bess:

> He stands watching her last pangs: the bridle is removed, and with a gaping mouth and wide-strained nostrils the wretched animal seems to devour the air — her flanks heave — a spasm

draws her round ribs and bends her powerful spine – her head is raised from earth; flexing her near leg, she rolls her forequarters from the ground; the off foreleg paws the road in vain – the trembling sinews slacken – they weaken, the power to rise is gone, another groan – she falls back prostrate – a sob – a groan – a gasp – a choking rattle – and she pours from her nostrils the spark of life, in a gush of blood, at the feet of her too-well-served master. Black Bess's heart is broken!

Miles's novel set the style for the numerous lives of Turpin that were to follow.

But it was not just novels which spread the Turpin legend. There were a number of stage adaptations of *Rookwood* immediately after the novel's publication, notably one at the Adelphi Theatre in London. And in this age, which so enjoyed melodrama, it was inevitable that Turpin's ride should be dramatised. *Turpin's Ride to York*, an equestrian drama, was written and performed soon after the publication of Ainsworth's novel, and, on the strength of comments by Ainsworth's biographer S. M. Ellis, was still being performed in abbreviated versions in music halls and circuses in the early twentieth century. Some sense of the piece's popularity is conveyed by featuring in Thomas Hardy's *Far from the Madding Crowd*, the dramatic interest for Hardy's story being that Sergeant Troy, the supposedly dead husband of the novel's heroine, Bathsheba Everdene, is playing the part of Turpin and is dismayed to discover that his wife is in the audience. Hardy, who is generally thought to have been accurate in his depiction of folklore and popular culture, gives a lively description of the performance, which is probably faithfully representative of those seen at country fairs in the second half of the nineteenth century. 'The fascination of the piece', according to Hardy, lay 'entirely in the action', and took in a dramatic entry by Turpin and Bess, a thrilling chase taking in a dramatic turnpike scene, the death of Tom King, and, of course, the death of the 'gallant and faithful Bess', whose body had to be carried off upon a shutter by twelve volunteers from the audience. After the performance, Bathsheba and one of her admirers, farmer Boldwood, fell into a conversation. Bathsheba asked:

> 'Have you seen the play of "Turpin's Ride to York"? Turpin was a real man, was he not?'
>
> 'O yes, perfectly true, all of it. Indeed, I think I've heard Jan Coggan say that a relation of his knew Tom King, Turpin's friend, quite well.'
>
> 'Coggan is rather given to strange stories connected with his relations, we must remember. I hope they can all be believed.'
>
> 'Yes, yes; we know Coggan. But Turpin is true enough ...'

By the mid-1870s, when *Far from the Madding Crowd* first appeared, the Turpin legend, with Black Bess, the ride to York, Tom King and all, was clearly part of the general culture of the country.

Let us turn to a now-forgotten medium for a demonstration of this point. From the early nineteenth century, middle-class children had played with toy theatre sets, enacting juvenile dramas in which they manipulated flat cut-out characters from cardboard cut-out sheets (sold, famously, at a penny plain and tuppence coloured), and used play texts produced specifically to accompany the figures from the cardboard sheets. By the 1830s one of the main publishers of these children's plays was Martin Skelt, probably originally a shoemaker by trade, who from the beginning of that decade began to buy up the stocks of other publishers of juvenile drama as their businesses failed, and then began publishing on his own account. He founded a family firm that achieved a prodigious output, and which also fought hard to establish a monopoly over the lucrative juvenile drama trade. The family, unfortunately, collectively did not have much of a head for business, and were drunks. Consequently, the firm collapsed in the 1860s, and Benjamin Skelt, one of several family members who had been in partnership with Martin, subsequently died in the workhouse like a character in some Vicorian melodrama. But among the Skelt family's products in their heyday, the 1840s, was a juvenile drama entitled *Richard Turpin the Highwayman, A Drama, in Two Acts, written expressly for, and adapted only to Skelt's Characters & Scenes in the Same*. This, based heavily on *Rookwood* and taking the ride to York as its central dramatic theme, vigorously reinforced the Turpin story as given by Ainsworth, complete with gipsies, Tom King and the dramatic death of Black Bess.

Skelt's juvenile dramas graced the middle-class drawing room, but literary products of a different nature, thought by many to be inappropriate for the young, were being read by boys and youths from the lower orders. It was not just novels that were on offer to the early Victorian reading public. In 1832 William Strange had published the first edition of *The Penny Story-Teller*, the precursor of a literary genre that was to become known as penny bloods, or, more commonly, penny dreadfuls, labels that characterised both the price of publications within this genre and the gist of their contents. William Strange may have provided the prototype for this form of publication, but it is generally accepted that their main begetter was Edward Lloyd, who after experimentation with other formats began printing serialised stories in the form of eight-page monthly magazines, sold for a penny. From the start, Lloyd published sensationalised accounts of crime. In 1836 he began publishing the *Lives of the most notorious Highwaymen, Footpads, etc* (presumably a pirated edition of Smith or Johnson's eighteenth-century works) in sixty episodes, and in the same year, on the strength of the success of this venture, he started to put out a 71-part *History of the Pirates of all Nations*, a title that again echoes early eighteenth-century publications. Lloyd published over 200 serials between the mid 1830s and the mid 1850s, among them plagiarised versions of Charles Dickens's works, usually with slightly altered titles, such as *The Penny Pickwick* and *Oliver Twiss*. But among the best selling of Lloyd's serials was Edward Viles's *Black Bess*, named after Turpin's horse, and the most successful of a number of serials that featured Ainsworth's reinvention of Turpin or highwaymen clearly modelled on that reinvention. The 'penny blood' format enjoyed considerable success over the second half of the nineteenth century. Lloyd's publications (which he was to disown and attempt to destroy when he became the head of a respectable newspaper empire) were joined by those of other companies, notably Edwin J. Brett's Newsagents Publishing Company, which was responsible for some of the most sensational serials of the period, notably *The Wild Boys of London: or the Children of the Night*, which, in 105 issues starting in 1860, recounted the story of a band of extremely deviant sewer-dwelling feral children. Among other characters to feature prominently in the penny bloods was the 'demon barber', Sweeney Todd, whose story was first put together in its modern form in *The String of Pearls: a Romance*, of 1846. And there was also the first character to popularise the vampire myth in England, the Yorkshire nobleman Sir Francis Varney, who was the central figure in another important early serial publication, *Varney the Vampire: or the Feast of Blood*.

This literature was rich with tales of highwaymen. One of the key sources in the study of penny dreadfuls and related literature is the collection made by the music hall performer Barry Ono (born Frederick Valentine Harrison in 1876). Ono had apparently loved these publications in his childhood, and as an adult set about collecting them, so that the Barry Ono collection is now regarded as one of the most important libraries of Victorian popular literature. The titles of some of the works brought together, many of them originating as weekly serials, are suggestive. They include *Black Hawke, the Highwayman*, published in nineteen weekly parts in 1866 by the Newsagents Publishing Company; *Black Wolf: or, the Boy Highwayman*, regarded as an unusually wellillustrated example of the genre, published in 1864; *Colonel Jack: or, the Life of a Highwayman*, which appeared around 1860; and *Captain Macheath, the Prince of the Highway*, a somewhat later publication of 1892. These works ran very much to a set format, their basic ethos being suggested in the title of a publication of 1852, *Gentleman Jack, or a Life on the Road. A Romance of Interest, abounding in hairbreath Escapes of the most exciting Characters*. They were directed primarily at boys and young men, but some of the titles suggest a female interest. There was, for example, *Jenny Diver, the female Highwayman*, which was published around 1851, *May Turpin, the Queen of the Road*, which appeared in 1864, and, a year later, *Nan Darrell: or, the Highwayman's Daughter*. And, of course, Dick Turpin was well represented in these publications. *Dick Turpin's celebrated Ride to York* came in 1850, and was followed by a stream of publications celebrating the ride, among them H. Milner's *Turpin's Ride to York: or, Bonny Black Bess. An Equestrian Drama in two Acts* published in 1885. Other popular publications collected by Ono and based on the Turpin story included *Turpin and Bess: a Romance of the Road*, dating from the early 1870s, and *Tyburn Dick: the Prince of Highwaymen*, this last published around 1884, possibly with children's stage scenes.

These works were not, nor intended to be, great art. *Tales of Highwaymen; or, Life on the road* was typical of the genre. It began appearing in weekly parts, published every Saturday, from January 1865 onwards. The first story to be serialised in this publication was 'Captain Macheath, the daring Highwayman. And the Black Rider of Hounslow', the illustration at the top of the first episode showing Macheath rescuing the heroine, Lady Nell, from the clutches of the Black Rider. This very much set the pattern for the stories that were to follow. There was minimal characterisation, but rather an emphasis on fast-moving action, and on the hero, who, while being on the wrong side of the law, in fact spent his time defeating villainy in its various forms. There was also frequently an undertone of sexual frisson in the stories. In issue 22, dated 10 June 1865, a new series began, 'Black Hugh: or, the Forty Thieves of London', which had as its danger-prone heroine another aristocrat, Lady May Cavendish. Four episodes into the story, Lady May is drugged by 'MacDuffy, the libertine', who has unequivocally dishonourable intentions in mind:

> After kissing her moist lips, he sat down again by the side of the
> bed, still holding her hand, preferring to feast his eyes upon the
> half-nude beauties of her superb form than to proceed at once to
> the gratification of his seminal appetites.

The delay was misjudged, for Lady May was rescued and Mac-
Duffy's 'seminal appetites' left ungratified. Shortly afterwards,
however, the heroine fell into the clutches of the Red Gipsies,
'the most libertine and blood-thirsty set of thieves in England',
although once again she was to survive intact. Action, melodrama and (usually aristocratic) women in distress ran through
this literature.

So it was hardly surprising that these penny dreadfuls
should have met with opposition, which focussed on their
propensity to turn boys to immorality and crime. These opinions, and the debates they engendered, have a curious resonance
for the modern reader. Today we are concerned about the
impact of video nasties and television violence on children, and,
most recently and specifically, on the effects of rap music on gun
possession and gun crime. For the Victorians, it was penny
dreadfuls and related forms of pulp fiction, and the characters
like Dick Turpin who were to be found in them, that were to
blame for juvenile delinquency.

This problem was pursued by James Greenwood, author of
The Seven Curses of London. In 1874 he published another work,
The Wilds of London, in which he wrote, among other things, on
the menace of 'the plague of poisonous literature'. For a
shilling, he recounted, he was able to buy a dozen 'nasty-feeling,
nasty-looking packets', each containing an episode of a story,
many of which can be found in the Ono collection, others

including *Admiral Tom, the King of the Boy Buccaneers*, *The Adventures of an Actress*, and *The Pretty Girls of London*. Greenwood gave a précis of the contents of his purchases, and in particular mentions one called *Hounslow Heath*. As Greenwood puts it:

> Picture: A poor wretch undergoing some frightful torture ... Dick Turpin figures in the story. Our number opens with an account of how he is beset by the officers of the law, how he blew out the brains of a Jew and sliced up others with his sword; but, over-powered by numbers, is about to yield, when in the nick of time he is rescued by some old friends who 'suddenly appear upon the scene'. Then Dick stops a stagecoach single-handed, and robs the passengers in his customary polite and graceful manner. Further on, it seems that the band of which Mr Turpin is the captain capture a person whom they suspect of planning to place them in the hands of justice. So they proceed to torture him as the picture on the front page faintly foretells.

Greenwood was convinced that literature of this sort promoted idleness, disrespect for the law and immorality. While he accepted that 'some of the weekly numbers contain more of obscenity and flagrant indecency than others', he argued that 'of the ingredients indicated they are one and all composed, and differ only in proportion and mixing'. The literature, he argued, was 'poison for the minds of girls and boys'.

Greenwood was not alone in his censures of this literary genre, and their influence on the young drew comments both from social commentators and from magistrates, although the allegedly harmful effects of pulp fiction were hotly contested, notably by G. K. Chesterton in his *Defence of Penny Dreadfuls*. This Victorian debate, like the modern one on the effects of television violence, remained unresolved; however, as so often happens when studying the history of crime and punishment, it leaves the modern observers with a depressing sense of déjà vu. More relevant for our purposes is how between 1834 and the 1870s the fictional Dick Turpin, who began his career as a literary hero in *Rookwood*, a conventional novel aimed at adults, should be turned, via the stories told about him and other highwaymen in the penny dreadfuls, into a potential corrupter of youth. The man hanged at York in April 1739 had, by the late nineteenth century, already cast a long shadow, and his reputation had undergone a number of mutations.

By the end of that century the old-style penny dreadful was a dying genre. Concern about the reading matter of the young was growing and, in 1879, respectability struck back with the founding of what was to become one of the most successful publications for adolescents ever, *The Boys Own Paper*, a journal originally published by the Religious Tract Society. Readership of *The Boys Own Paper* was to become overwhelmingly middle class, and something akin to the old penny dreadfuls continued to be read avidly by the errand boys and others whose reading habits so worried James Greenwood. But now a more wholesome form of boys' literature was being created, and this blossomed over the early twentieth century. Tales of Dick Turpin and other highwaymen were still being read by boys, but their moral content had changed. Consider, for example, the thoughts expressed in the foreword of Arthur L. Hayward's *The Boys Book of Highwaymen*, published in 1931:

Romantic as the highwaymen were, and bright as was the glamour cast about their adventures, it must never for one moment be forgotten that the men who haunted the roads and lonely woods were rogues who richly deserved the punishment that almost invariably overtook them. They were cowards, too; for what more cowardly than to present a pistol at the head of an unsuspecting traveller and tell him you will press the trigger unless he hands you his purse. For that was all the highwaymen did. So let us read their stories and enjoy their adventures, without making heroes of them.

And the stories that were told were now sanitised, compared to those recounted in the Victorian penny dreadfuls: less gore, less wanton violence and certainly no semi-naked Lady May Cavendishes. The image of the English highwayman in general, and that of Dick Turpin in particular, had changed yet again.

And it was to keep on changing, and was to adapt itself to all available media as the twentieth century unfolded. The Turpin legend has proved durable, and has undergone a number of mutations since the decisive refashioning wrought by Ainsworth. Probing these reformulations, we find Dick Turpin appearing variously as a threat to the morals of the nation's youth, as a heroic character played in fishnet tights as a pantomime principal boy, as a Staffordshire pottery figure and as the hero in the Victorian children's toy theatre. Pursuing the progress of the Turpin legend leads us down some unexpected cultural sidestreets.

We shall examine these twentieth-century mutations in due course. At the beginning of the twenty-first, we can get information about Turpin, like almost everything else, from the Internet. And what surfing the net demonstrates most clearly is how Turpin has been appropriated by that major phenomenon of our current understanding of the past, the heritage industry. Thus York, where Turpin died and a city that counts tourism as a major factor in its economy, makes much of its links with the highwaymen. Websites featuring York, such as that of *www.leisureyork.co.uk*, carry pictures of Turpin's grave, while the City's deservedly famous Castle Museum, once the county gaol where Turpin was incarcerated before execution, admits visitors into what is publicised as the condemned cell where Turpin spent his last few days. Another York attraction, the York Dungeon ('Welcome to a very bloody history: yours') has among its other dramatic scenes a life-sized tableau of Turpin, mounted on Black Bess, holding up a stage coach. The website for Bishopthorpe Palace near York mentions a former archbishop of York with a questionable reputation, Lancelot Blackburne, who, we are told, employed Turpin as his butler. More generally, Turpin is frequently mentioned in descriptions of York, sometimes, despite the fact that he was a native of Essex, being described as the city's most famous son. Other Yorkshire towns also claim or imply an association with Turpin. Thus a website for the small town of Selby asserts that drinking in the town's old local pubs will give the visitor 'a feel for the history of English legends like Dick Turpin, the famous highwayman'.

The image of Turpin is invoked by numerous websites dealing with localities outside Yorkshire. Again, the connection claimed is sometimes an oblique one: a Nottinghamshire Heritage website, for example, merely points out that the old Great North Road, 'once haunted by the highwayman Dick Turpin', passes through Retford in the county. More frequently, and with varying degrees of plausibility, assertions are made by a number of localities that Turpin operated or hid in nearby heaths or woodlands. Towns or areas making this claim include (and this list is far from comprehensive) Basingstoke, Shooters Hill in south-east London, Hounslow Heath, and Iver Heath in Buckinghamshire.

Other sites make a more specific reference. A website charting the history of the River Fleet in London, mentioning Newgate prison, claims that Dick Turpin lived in the area and (conflating Turpin with Jack Sheppard) that Turpin was famous for escaping from Newgate gaol by 'a climbing feat of great agility'. Specific crimes are sometimes referred to, so that Turpin, for example, is reputed to have held up and murdered a man on a heath between Dunston and Nocton in Lincolnshire. Sometimes Turpin's former presence in an area is perpetuated by his or Black Bess's ghost. Hence Turpin's ghost is supposed to ride on the spectre of Black Bess up Trapps Hill in Essex, with the ghost of an old woman he had tortured clinging to his back. The ghosts of Turpin and Bess are also reputed to ride along Weathercock (alias Woodcock) Lane in Apsley Guise in Bedfordshire, local legend claiming that Turpin had been allowed to use the local manor house as a hideout after he had discovered that its owner had murdered his daughter and her unsuitable lover.

One of the more curious examples of this use of the past is on a website constructed by the British Sausage Appreciation Society to celebrate an event which has not, perhaps, so far achieved the recognition it deserves, British Sausage Appreciation Week. Among the other little-known facts it drew upon to bolster the image of the British sausage, it declared that 'legendary highwayman Dick Turpin was known to moonlight as a butcher making sausages from the finest meats in Epping Forest'. Although it seems reasonable that, as a butcher, Turpin would have made sausages, documentary evidence on this point and their quality is entirely lacking. Everyone, it seems, wants a piece of Dick Turpin.

The mobilisation of Turpin by modern website creators should not obscure the existence of older Turpin traditions, which demonstrate the aura of romance that was felt to surround the post-*Rookwood* Turpin. Writing in 1908, Charles G. Harper, more sceptical about these matters than many, mentioned a 'Dick Turpin's Stone' which stood in 'an evil-smelling ditch that receives the drainage of the neighbouring pigsties' between Keevil and Bulkington in Wiltshire. This stone was inscribed with writing that could be deciphered as 'Dick Turpin's dead and gone/ This stone's set up to think upon'. Harper noted caustically that 'brake-loads of Wiltshire archaeologists visited the spot in the summer, when county antiquaries archaeologise, and, braving typhoid fever, have descended into the ditch and sought to unravel the mystery of this Sphinx: without result'. Such traditions were widespread and well established from a fairly early date. William Nobbs, the parish clerk of Welwyn in Hertfordshire, writing in the early nineteenth century, alluded to a tradition that Turpin and

James Whitney, a notorious and Hertfordshire-born highway-man executed in 1694, operated in a 'Great Wood' on the fringes of the parish. There was once a causeway of white stones at Peckham Rye in south-east London that was known as 'Dick's Ride' on the strength of a tradition that Turpin had ridden there. The author of a late nineteenth-century parish history of Naburn, a village to the south of York, reported that 'I have heard it remarked that perhaps Dick Turpin, the high-wayman, was a native of Naburn as we have some fields called Turpin's Garths', although he exercised some scepticism in noting that Turpin was a fairly common surname in that part of Yorkshire.

The places currently most frequently claiming Turpin asso-ciations are pubs. There are, of course, a fair number of public houses called the Dick Turpin in England, including one on Moorcroft Road in York, which is within striking distance of the site of Turpin's execution. But interestingly, as well as its cachet for pubs in England, Dick Turpin's name has been adopted as symbolising Englishness among owners of bars abroad. There is a Dick Turpin English-style pub on the rue de Loup in Bordeaux, much frequented by students, and selling draught English beer and attempting to introduce the French to the delights of jacket potatoes with cheddar cheese. There is also a Dick Turpin pub, with a nineteenth-century-style depiction of a highwayman on a black horse for its sign, in the Swedish town (in effect a suburb of Stockholm) of Solna. Perhaps even more surprisingly, there is a restaurant called the Dick Turpin on the waterfront at San Remo in Italy, where one diner reports being very impressed by the calzone, a dish probably not much in vogue in early eighteenth-century Essex.

To return to England, the public house with the most strongly claimed Turpin associations is the Spaniards in Hampstead. An 'Old Hampstead' website, indeed, in an interesting application of misinformation technology, tells us that Turpin was actually born in the pub, that he had a tunnel dug between this inn and another pub to help him evade his pursuers, and that he stabled Black Bess in a nearby toll house. A Campaign for Real Ale North London Branch issue for July/August 2000 repeats the claim that Turpin had been born in the pub, 'son of the then landlord John Turpin', adding that Turpin would watch passing coaches from an upstairs room, now named the Turpin Bar, and that the main bar has on display a bullet fired by Turpin at a Royal Mail coach. But another website, that of Pubs.com, rather dashes these claims for Turpin connections at the Spaniards: the building in which the pub is located dates from the late sixteenth century, but it did not become used as an inn until the mid eighteenth century, a little after Turpin's death in 1739.

Such a taste for accuracy is rare, and there are, indeed, so many pubs alleging Turpin associations that if all their claims were true, the career of England's most famous highwayman would have been passed in a combination of perpetual motion and a permanent alcoholic haze. However, there are some establishments where the claim can be substantiated. The Ferry Inn at Brough notes modestly that it was frequented by Turpin towards the end of his career, a claim that is based on fact rather than legend. Other Yorkshire pubs claiming connections with Turpin do so on less certain grounds. The website for the Beverley Arms Hotel claims that 'history links this hotel to the highwayman Dick Turpin', presumably on the basis of his stay in the town in late 1738. The Bay Horse at Barlby near Selby is at least at the right end of Yorkshire to have been within the orbit of Turpin's horse-dealing activities, but the 'local folk-lore' that Turpin lived in the inn while laying low during times when he was being pursued is far fetched (the relevant website, intriguingly, notes that documentation proving this connection was lost in a fire at the York Records Office). The Golden Fleece at Thirsk claims to have been 'once the haunt of Dick Turpin', although no basis for this assertion is given. In a news-paper article published in 1952 it was also claimed that Dick Turpin spent a night at the Three Horse Shoes in Brierley, near Barnsley, although closer associations are claimed with John (sic) Nevison, while another South Yorkshire Turpin location is the Crown Hotel at Bawtry, where apparently the sound of the hoof-beats of Black Bess's ghost are regularly heard.

Beyond Yorkshire, there is a fine geographical spread of pubs claiming to have been frequented, or at least visited, by Turpin. Many of these, perhaps with better hopes of accuracy than most of the others, are to be found in the London area and in districts that were, in the eighteenth century, on the capital's peripheries. The Anchor Inn, Shepperton, claims to have been a regular haunt of Turpin, a pistol inscribed 'Dick's Friend' having apparently been discovered in the rafters. A pair of Turpin's pistols are alleged to be immured within the walls of Ye Olde King's Head in Chigwell, Essex, and here too there was reputed to be a tunnel running out of the inn's cellar to aid Turpin when he had to escape pursuers. Turpin is said to have hidden in the cellars of the Flask Inn in Highgate, and to have been a visitor to the London Apprentice in Isleworth and the Trafalgar tavern in Greenwich – this last institution, if it existed as a public house in Turpin's time, presumably operating under another title, given that the battle after which it was named occurred in 1805. Turpin is also reputed to have drunk in the White House on Hackney Marshes, to have planned robberies at the Catherine Wheel in east London (destroyed by fire in 1895), to have been associated with the White Swan at Aldgate (demolished in the first half of the twentieth century), and to have frequented the Old Bull and Bush in Hampstead.

Another grouping of pubs where one can at least see the logic of claims to a Turpin connection are those which are on, or close to, the route Ainsworth plotted for him during the epic (and, let us remind ourselves, entirely fictional) ride from London to York. Thus there are rumours that Turpin stayed at the Fox in Grantham, a story that he spent a night at the George in Huntingdon, and a legend that Turpin shoed his horse the wrong way round so as to confuse his pursuers in a now-demolished inn located on a site currently occupied by the Crown and Woolpack in Connington. There were also strong Turpin associations with the Jockey House near Ordsall on the Great North Road, and apparently in the Edwardian era wagonettes brought tourists there to see the inn where the great highwayman had hidden. Turpin was also reputed to have used the Red Lion Inn at Digswell Hill on the Great North Road in Hertfordshire, where his seat by the fireside was once proudly displayed to visitors. He also reputedly stayed at the George Hotel in Buckden, again on the Great North Road, yet another site that is allegedly still haunted by his ghost.

Further afield, there are numerous claims for associations with Turpin made by pubs in areas where he is known to have operated very briefly, or not at all. Such claims have been made for the Half Way Inn (halfway, that is, between London and Bristol), the George Hotel at Wallingford, where he is supposed to have stayed, the Blue Bell Inn at Levenshulme, where according to legend Turpin had been a regular visitor, and the Old White Hart in Godalming, where, more modestly, he is reputed to have spent the night on one occasion. In Leicestershire, we find the Bell Inn at Stilton claiming to have been a regular haunt of Dick Turpin. Apparently he stayed there for three years, which suggests that historians have left a lengthy gap in his career undetected, and he had a piece cut out of a roof beam so that he could escape quickly without bumping his head. It was also claimed (in another echo of one of the stories told about the Spaniards in Hampstead) that Turpin also facilitated his escapes by using a secret passage which connected the Bell to another pub in the village, the Angel. Even more extravagant claims are made for the Cock at Sibson, near Hinckley. We find that this inn was a haunt of Turpin's in the 1730s, that he lived with his parents in a cottage in the area, and that Black Bess was kept in a clearing in nearby Lindley Wood. Another account describes the pub as Turpin's favourite hideaway, and has him hiding in the chimney in the inn's bar when pursuers came too close. Turpin, described in the relevant website as a Yorkshireman who was born in York, was also reputed to have frequently used the Old Swan Inn at Wroughton-on-the-Green in Buckingham as his base. The Anchor at Catshill, Lower Stonall, also enjoys Turpin associations, although the author of this website, another of that minority with an agreeable regard for historical accuracy, points out that the pub was built in 1797, nearly sixty years after Turpin's death. Turpin is also reputed to have visited the Bell Inn at Kennet, near Newmarket in Cambridgeshire and Ye Olde Leathern Bottel at Wednesbury in the Black Country, and to have stayed at the Swan Inn at Aston Munslow in south Staffordshire. The Three Tuns in Cambridge was recorded as possessing a hat, coat, doublet, mask, cravat, spurs and pistol allegedly left behind by Turpin after he evaded officers whilst staying at the inn, while rebuilding operations undertaken many years ago at the Coach and Horses public house in Clerkenwell apparently revealed a valise with 'R. Turpin' cut into its side.

So Dick Turpin, over two and a half centuries after his death, and over a century and a half after being reincarnated by William Harrison Ainsworth, is still very much with us. His image is a powerful one, especially to those seeking to evoke an aura of past glamour and adventure for their local area or their local pub, even for British sausages. The progress of that image over the twentieth century, to which we shall turn next, shows how the broader culture has constantly found new ways to appropriate our most famous highwayman, and has constantly developed and reinforced his legend.

Although the old-style penny bloods and penny dreadfuls may have fallen out of fashion by 1900, tales of Turpin and other highwaymen continued to figure prominently in boys' adventure stories. Indeed, Turpin's name was sufficiently evocative for the Aldin Publishing Company to issue a weekly publication, simply entitled *Dick Turpin*, of which 182 weekly issues were published between April 1902 and September 1909, and for

Newnes to publish the *Dick Turpin Library*, which appeared in 138 issues between 1922 and 1930. The *Thriller Picture Library*, published in the 1950s, regularly featured Dick Turpin among its heroes, along with other such familiar figures as Robin Hood and Claude Duval and new ones like Battler Britton and Daring of the Mounties. Arthur Geoffrey Campion, one of the most celebrated British children's strip cartoonists of the 1950s and 1960s, was responsible for two Dick Turpin strips, one of them in the popular *Knockout Fun Book*, and he also drew a strip featuring a highwaywoman as heroine for the short-lived girls' magazine *Poppet*.

But children's magazines and comics were not the only medium through which the young of twentieth-century Britain, and indeed the English-speaking world more generally, were introduced to the theme of highwaymen. Many people over fifty remember reading at school, and possibly having to learn, a poem by Alfred Noyes entitled 'The Highwayman'. The first few stanzas of this poem are especially evocative. The first tells how a highwayman rides up to an 'old inn-door' on a blustery, moonlit night, and the poem then continues:

He'd a French cocked-hat on his forehead, a bunch of lace at
  his chin,
A coat of the claret velvet, and breeches of brown doe-skin.
They fitted with never a wrinkle. His boots were up to the thigh.
And he rode with a jewelled twinkle,
      His pistol butts a-twinkle,
His rapier hilt a-twinkle, under the jewelled sky.

Over the cobbles he clattered and clashed in the dark inn-yard.

He tapped with his whip on the shutters, but all was locked and
barred.
He whistled a tune to the window, and who should be waiting
there
But the landlord's black-eyed daughter,
Bess, the landlord's daughter,
Plaiting a dark red love-knot into her long black hair.

Noyes's 'The Highwayman' was, in fact, a short tale of love,
jealousy and death. The highwayman here, as surely as the
Claude Duval of Frith's painting, was a figure designed to rein-
force the romantic image. He is a dashing figure, complete with
French cocked-hat, lace at his throat, doe-skin breeches, thigh
boots, pistols and sword. Bess, the black-eyed daughter of the
landlord of an inn (and is this a conscious attempt to evoke
Black Bess?) that the highwayman frequents is in love with him,
which inflames the jealousy of Tim the ostler, who holds a passion for Bess. In the hopes of removing his highwayman rival,
Tim informs on the couple, soldiers arrive and tie Bess up,
standing her up in a parody of a soldier at attention, a musket by
her side, and await the highwayman's return. Bess, willing to
sacrifice herself to save her love from ambush, manages to free a
hand from her bonds and fires the musket, killing herself but
warning her love as he comes into view. He rides off, but is shot
down by the troops, the poem ending with lines describing how
the couple's ghosts still haunt the inn and the road leading to it.

Alfred Noyes, in his autobiography, expressed surprise at
how the poem had become so successful, and told how he had
written it at the beginning of the twentieth century, as a young
man just down from Oxford. He was staying in an appropriate

place, Bagshot Heath, and wrote his most famous poem in just two days, his autobiography also noting that his original inspiration for the piece had probably come from reading *Rookwood* as a boy. Noyes was subsequently to write a poem entitled 'Dick Turpin's Ride', at the end of which Turpin meets the spectre of his future dead self. Noyes's 'The Highwayman', widely reprinted in anthologies and schoolbooks, and the basis for two cantatas, was one of the most powerful forces helping to keep the romantic image of the highwayman alive.

Noyes's poem is well known, but a mass of other works were preserving both the romantic image of the highwayman and the heroic status of Dick Turpin. From the mid nineteenth century the image of Turpin was preserved through a variety of media. There were numerous sets of prints, usually derived from the plot of *Rookwood*, showing scenes from Turpin's life or from the ride to York. One such, for example, widely dispersed in the nineteenth century, shows Turpin on Black Bess leaping over a donkey cart, dismayed at the sight of a gibbet on the road to York, plunging into the River Ouse on Bess as his pursuers fire pistols at him, and, finally, standing devastated at the spectacle of a dying Black Bess. There were also toys, such as a board game inspired by Turpin's ride to York, probably dating from the late nineteenth century, and a shooting game from about 1950 in which children could shoot down a cardboard figure of Turpin with a pop-gun . Turpin, naturally enough, featured in a cigarette-card set celebrating famous highwaymen, and the figure of Turpin, or perhaps of highwaymen more generally, was widely used in advertisements and brand names for a wide variety of products. There were probably other artefacts, examples of which have by now largely been lost: a recent auction catalogue, for example, had as one lot a Dick Turpin table cigarette lighter.

One of the more enduring sources for the popularity of Dick Turpin was the porcelain figures that served as ornaments in many British homes. Turpin had long featured among these, and as late as 1989 Royal Doulton issued a figure of Turpin, clad in the by now traditional boots, frock coat, tricorn hat and face mask riding on a rearing Black Bess. This modern figure contrasts with some earlier designs, notably a Staffordshire figure issued in the mid nineteenth century which depicts a Turpin, standing eleven inches high, dressed very much in the style of the illustrations of highwaymen found in the popular literature of the period. Another Staffordshire product of the same era was a set of two flatback figures depicting Turpin and Tom King, examples of which still turn up in good condition at auctions. The most common items to survive, however, are examples of a Turpin character jug produced by Royal Doulton between 1940 and 1960. This has Turpin, older in this depiction than Turpin actually was when he died, mustachioed and smiling, available in two sizes, six and a half inches and three and a half inches high. Another tangentially related, and modern, product is a rare piece of Turpin pornographia. The 'Adult Novelties' advertised by the firm Gifts4Anyone include an item entitled Dick Turpin ('ideal as novelty gifts and for that girls' night or a hen party'), which takes the form of a six and a half-inch erect penis topped by a tricorn hat, masked, and with a pair of pistols at its sides.

The Turpin legend was also kept alive in that most traditional of media, folksong. Roughly at the time of Turpin's execution, a broadside ballad was published entitled 'Turpin's

Rant'. This told the story of how Turpin, while riding over Hounslow Heath, met with a lawyer travelling alone. Turpin asked the lawyer if he was not afraid of being robbed by the famous Dick Turpin, to which the lawyer replied that he had his money hidden in his cape. The two travelled on together, and a little later, in a suitably secluded place, Turpin robbed the lawyer. This song survived in the oral tradition for over two centuries, changing a little, and becoming known most commonly under the title 'Turpin Hero', a term used in its chorus (as one version has it, 'For I'm the hero, the Turpin hero, I am the great Dick Turpin Ho'). Its popularity can be inferred from its having been collected in Lincolnshire, in Sussex, in the upper Thames Valley, and in Nova Scotia. The song, in an interesting demonstration of the pervasiveness of the Dick Turpin legend, suggested to James Joyce the title for his prototype for *Portrait of the Artist as a Young Man,* namely *Stephen Hero.* There are other folksongs featuring Turpin, while there was a massive vogue for printed broadside ballads about Turpin and Black Bess in the wake of the enthusiastic reception of *Rookwood.* Moving to twentieth-century popular music, we find that 'Bold Dick Turpin' was the title of one of the lesser-known compositions of the Lancashire songster-cum-ukelele-strummer, George Formby.

By the early twentieth century the folksong was, of course, in decline. But is no surprise, and yet further evidence of how the fictional Dick Turpin could adapt to and perpetuate itself through new media, that the Turpin legend provided material for that most twentieth-century of art forms, the cinema. There may have been short movies based on Turpin and the ride to York among the first, and now largely forgotten, products of the early British silent cinema. Certainly 1906 witnessed the release of a film entitled *Dick Turpin's Ride to York*, which featured an early appearance by Moore Marriott, who was to be best remembered for his later participation in Will Hay comedies. In 1922 a film of the same title appeared, the product of the British director Maurice Elvey, who was to direct some 150 movies in a career which ran from 1913 to 1957. But the first film using the Turpin story to figure prominently in film histories was a 1925 version entitled *Dick Turpin* and starring Tom Mix, the then superstar of western movies, and also featuring an early appearance by a then virtually unknown actress, Carole Lombarde. Mix, an energetic performer, expert horseman and fearless stuntman, appeared in numerous films (his filmography runs to about 302 items) which in the 1920s created many of the conventions of the western movie genre. His *Dick Turpin* was very much in this mode, a fast-moving and stunt-filled yarn lasting seventy minutes. The movie featured on 28 May 1925 at the opening night of the famous Fox Fullerton Theater in California, which, at the time of its construction, represented the height of Hollywood glamour. It was shown as part of an evening of varied entertainments that included, appropriately, a performance of Alfred Noyes's poem 'The Highwayman' set to music, a demonstration of the piece's widespread popularity.

The Turpin story figured in a number of later films. An interesting variation on the Turpin theme came in 1933 with *Dick Turpin*, in which the ride to York was made to avoid an enforced marriage. This was a typical British costume drama of the period, although it helped make a star of its leading man, Victor McLagan. The year 1965 witnessed the release of *The Legend of the Young Dick Turpin*, the title role performed by David

Weston, at that time a rising star who had, a year previously, played the hero confronting Vincent Price's villain in *The Masque of the Red Death*, while another participant was William Franklyn, who a year later was to appear in a rather different film, Roman Polanski's *Cul de Sac*. About a decade earlier, Dick Turpin had provided the subject matter for one of a number of short 'featurettes' produced by Hammer Films. This helped continue the highwayman's romantic image, with Turpin, according to the opening titles, being a 'bold, gallant adventurer with an eye for a fine horse or a pretty girl'. The highwayman as hero was also a theme central to a film of 1951, released in the United States as *The Lady and the Bandit* and in Britain as *Dick Turpin's Ride*, in which the hero sacrifices his life to avenge his father and save his wife. This romantic image was further fostered by another 1951 film, *The Highwayman*, based not on the Turpin myth but inspired by Alfred Noyes's poem. In this film, essentially a low-budget action movie, the highwayman was a seventeenth-century English nobleman who took to the road in order to right wrongs.

In 1974, however, Dick Turpin's memory was awarded a major accolade when the highwayman became the hero of a Carry On movie. *Carry On Dick*, directed by Gerald Thomas and the twenty-sixth film in the Carry On series, used the Turpin legend as a hook for ninety-one minutes of typical Carry On humour, the tone being set by the film's poster, which announced that 'Dick Turpin carries on with his flintlock cocked!'. Most of the regular members of the Carry On team were involved. Turpin ('more commonly referred to as Big Dick') was played by Sid James, who also masqueraded as the Rector, the Reverend Flasher, of St Michael's Church in the village of Upper Denture, on the York Road (production values are indicated by the visible presence of a twentieth-century war memorial in the churchyard). Barbara Windsor played Harriet, a female highwayman who worked with Turpin and maintained the disguise of being the Reverend Flasher's maidservant by day. Turpin's other associate, Tom (presumably an echo of Tom King), was played by Peter Butterworth. Kenneth Williams played Captain Desmond Fancy, a Bow Street Runner who was out to get Turpin, and whose bungling and misadventures form much of the plot of the film, while the head of the Bow Street Runners, Sir Roger Daley, was played by Bernard Bresslaw. Other characters included Jack Douglas as Sergeant Jock Strap of the Bow Street Runners, Hattie Jacques as the Reverend Flasher's faithful housekeeper, Martha, and Joan Sims as Madame Desiree, proprietor of a troupe of young women (Les Oiseaux de Paradis) who perform exotic tableaux in Upper Denture's local hostelry, the Cock Inn.

Fortunately, we need not worry about the plot or the humour of *Carry On Dick*. What is of interest is that once again we have the image of a Turpin who, while by no means dashing or romantic (putting Sid James in the Turpin role, whatever the actor's many talents, rather precluded that) outwits the forces of the law, who are throughout portrayed as ineffective and blundering. The story opens, indeed, by being set in the 1750s, when the newly formed Bow Street Runners were operating in the face of a crime wave, Turpin being the only criminal to consistently escape their clutches. The film's interest is that it demonstrates how the Turpin story could be adjusted for yet another cultural purpose, and how, once again, Dick Turpin, in however attenuated a form, is an instantly recognisable figure for most of the population of Britain.

The Turpin story made an easy transition from cinema to television, most memorably in the series *Dick Turpin*. Released by London Weekend Television early in 1979, it was an immediate success, and was to run over four series totalling thirty-one half-hour episodes. Written by Paul Carpenter, it was produced by Paul Knight and Sydney Cole, and starred Richard O'Sullivan. His portrayal of the highwayman proved a major success, perpetuating the image of Turpin as a gallant Robin Hood-type figure, his authority-defying adventures never really harming anybody. The series produced a number of spin-offs, among them two novellas, *Dick Turpin* and *Turpin and Swiftnicks*, published in 1979 and 1980 respectively, and at least one release of a *Dick Turpin Annual*, copies of which, containing stories, comic strip art, and star profiles, survive from 1980. The television *Dick Turpin* series was important in providing yet another repackaging of the Turpin legend, making it available in the most important medium of the late twentieth century, and, in particular, introducing Dick Turpin to yet another generation of young people.

Throughout the twentieth century, however, the highwayman myth, if not the legend of Dick Turpin *per se*, was being preserved in literature. There were a vast number of novels, for both adults and children alike, about highwaymen, and in 1990 another important cultural milestone was reached: if Dick Turpin could inspire a Carry On film, so the myth of the romantic highwayman could inspire a Mills and Boon novel, *Highwayman Bride* by Janet Edmonds. The bride in question is Lady Araminta Wareham, an attractive aristocratic twenty-year-old, whose prospects of marriage are limited by a poor dowry and a feisty nature. Due to family circumstances she agrees to an arranged marriage to the foppish Marquess of Cosenham, for whom she conceives a deep loathing. Shortly before the wedding, Araminta is robbed on the highway by a dashing highwayman who gives her a kiss that leaves a lasting impression on the young girl. She decides, on her wedding night, to run away from her hated groom, and turns highwayman, meeting in due course the man who had robbed and kissed her, who is none other than the dashing highwayman of great local fame, Jack Ranton. She falls heavily in love with him, but the love remains unconsummated (any other outcome would be too much even for a Mills and Boon novel of 1990), and is eventually captured and imprisoned, her disguise as a young man holding good. She is released from prison by Lord Cosenham, who then takes her back to his country house, professing himself anxious to consummate the marriage. Araminta, still thinking such a development undesirable, awaits her husband in a locked bedroom, holding in her hand a poker with which she intends to kill him, when the door opens, and who should come in but her true love, the highwayman Jack Ranton. It transpires that Cosenham's foppishness was a front, and that he, in fact, is Ranton, and has been robbing the highway and smuggling contraband in order to relieve the boredom of eighteenth-century aristocratic life. The marriage is promptly consummated to the mutual satisfaction of Araminta and Cosenham/Ranton on a rug in front of an open fire, and we are left to assume that the hero will give up both his criminal exploits and his foppishness, and that the two will live happily ever after. Yet again, the highwayman motif proves itself capable of constant refashioning.

11. *Refashioning the Turpin image took on a new turn in 1974 when the movie* Carry on Dick *was produced, with Sid James starring as Turpin (© London Features International Ltd: By kind permission).*

12. *The publication of* Rookwood *in 1834 was followed by several dramatizations of the Turpin story, and Dick Turpin continues to be the main character in theatrical productions. This is part of the publicity materials for one such, produced by the York-based Riding Lights Theatre Company in 2000 (By kind permission of the Riding Lights Theatre Company).*

And as if to demonstrate that assertion, at the time of writing the latest incarnation of the Turpin myth is establishing itself on the amateur stage. As we have noted, dramatisations of the Turpin story, and especially of his ride to York, appeared immediately after the publication of *Rookwood*, and continued over the nineteenth and into the early twentieth century. By that point, Turpin was figuring on the music-hall stage. A sketch entitled 'Dick Turpin's Ride to York' was performed for many years by two now-forgotten music-hall stars, the brothers Fred and Claude Ginnett, while another performer, R. A. Roberts, used the theme in an impressive one-man show in which he made a number of rapid costume changes in a sketch involving seven or eight characters depicting Turpin playing a game of hide and seek with the officers pursuing him. More recently, the Turpin theme has been reworked in an entertainment presented in 2001 by York's Riding Lights Theatre Company, who gave a lengthy run in their Friargate Theatre to 'a swinging theatre sensation' entitled *Dick Turpin*. This was publicised as 'a break-neck, eye-popping piece of music theatre – a night to keep you in breathless suspense until the final curtain'. And, in a conscious nod at the Turpin legend, this publicity also reminded its readers that 'ever since his last drop at York's Knavesmire, Dick Turpin has been riding through the moonlit world of our mythology – glamorous, chivalrous, a big hit with the ladies'.

But for the final modern refashioning of the Turpin legend so far to emerge it is essential to go to the English pantomime. In 1995 Paul Reakes, author of a number of such works, published a pantomime, intended for amateur dramatic societies, simply entitled *Dick Turpin*. The cast list will hold few surprises for anybody familiar with the genre. There is a pantomime dame, Dame Dollop, owner of the farm where much of the action takes place. There is Katie Cuddlesome, a milkmaid with rosy cheeks and a pert manner, who is enamoured with the glamour of tales of Dick Turpin, and her admirer, the gormless but loveable Billy Bumpkin. There is Parson Goodfellow, who doubles as the master criminal, Mr X; Lord Lootalot, a caricature of an eighteenthcentury aristocrat, with a florid complexion, fine silk waistcoats, and gout, and his daughter Caroline, the romantic interest. Inevitably Daisy the pantomime cow makes an appearance, as do Nick and Nab, the comic Bow Street Runners, and a number of other characters. And then, of course, there is Dick Turpin, the principal boy, played, according to the conventions of the English pantomime, by a young woman. The playwright prescribes that Turpin should be played as a romanticised version of the highwayman, 'with a bold swagger and a magnificent pair of legs', and sets out his ideas on Turpin's costume: black fishnet tights, thigh boots, shortened brocade waistcoat, white fullsleeved blouse with a fancy jabot, black cloak, black tricorn hat, and a black halfmask with hair tied back with a black bow.

The plot of *Dick Turpin* the pantomime cannot detain us long. Briefly, Turpin is adopting the disguise of a farm labourer working on Dame Dollop's farm while he is attempting to discover who is committing dreadful crimes and attributing them to him (it is, of course, Mr X and his associates, Smash and Grab). Turpin uncovers the conspiracy, and in the process he and Caroline fall in love, and Katie Cuddlesome, deprived of her hero, decides that Billy Bumpkin, who has long admired her, is not such a bad bet after all. The full panoply of conventions surrounding the English pantomime is evoked in the piece, with song-and-dance routines, *double entendres* from the dame, chases, lots of business with Daisy the Cow, and ample room left for the cast to make joking allusions to stars of stage, screen, the popular music industry and to local football teams.

So there are a dazzling range of representations of Dick Turpin that the unstoppable progress of his legend after the publication of *Rookwood* has created: representations that are encapsulated in practically all forms of media, among them the novel, the boys' comic paper, the theatre, the toy theatre, folk-song, Staffordshire pottery, the music hall, cinema, television and, most recently, the pantomime. The net result of this process has been to establish an image of Turpin that is best summed up in York's Riding Lights Theatre Company's publicity notes for their own production on the Turpin theme: '... glamorous, chivalrous, a big hit with the ladies'. This, of course, has absolutely no connection with the 'real' Turpin of documentary history. Does this matter? Should people be told about it?

DICK TURPIN *and the* MEANING *of* HISTORY

There are a lot of Dick Turpins. There is what we might optimistically refer to as the real one. That is, the son of John and Mary Turpin, born in Essex in 1705, who was a butcher by trade, drifted into crime, became a notorious high-wayman, and was eventually executed at York in 1739. But this is not the Turpin who is lodged in the public mind. The public's Turpin is not the historically verifiable pock-marked thug. Rather, he is a romantic, courageous, daredevil figure, elegantly clad and handsome, robbing the rich to help the poor, defying corrupt authority, and riding a faithful mare called Black Bess on whom he made his epic journey to York. It is this Turpin who has stalked the pages of novels, nineteenth-century penny dreadfuls and twentieth-century boys' comics. It is this Turpin, instantly recognisable, who appeared in equestrian spectacles, in films, in television programmes, in a modern pantomime, and on the signs outside the many pubs that bear Turpin's name, from York to San Remo with Bordeaux in between.

The popular Turpin is more than an individual man. Within this 'constructed' Turpin is enshrined that more general figure, the English highwayman. Few people nowadays have heard of James Hind, Claude Duval, William Nevison or the other figures who once so fascinated the popular imagination and whose biographies were constantly reworked in chapbooks and in collections of lives of the highwaymen. So highwaymen in general are attributed with those same qualities that we like to feel are encapsulated in Turpin: the daring, the elegance, the gallantry to ladies, and the tendency, Robin Hood-like, to rob the rich to help the poor.

The rehabilitation of Turpin's image was firmly established by the early twentieth century. S. M. Ellis, William Harrison Ainsworth's biographer, writing in 1911, applauding Ainsworth's powers as a creative writer, reminded his readers that the story of Turpin's ride to York, 'implicitly believed to be fact by thousands of persons', existed only in Ainsworth's imagination. Ellis continued:

The story of Dick's dashing ride will live forever – conjoined with the name of his matchless mare, Black Bess. All along the Great North Road the legend is truth; every village through which the highwayman galloped (in the imagination of Ainsworth) during that famous ride has its own peculiar tale and relic of Turpin's feat. From Tottenham to Ware – from Huntingdon to Stamford – from Newark to York – a volume of Turpinian anecdotes could be collected from innkeepers and ostlers; here, you may learn how Turpin refreshed his mare with strong ale and see the actual tankard he used; and there, how he leaped the five-barred toll-gate! And yet the ride never took place, and the splendid mare never died at the moment of victory within sight of the towers of York. The death of Black

Bess makes painful reading, but she, after all, only lived in shadowland ...

The Turpin legend gained a powerful hold very quickly, and, as
Ellis makes clear, it is remarkable how a totally fictitious exploit
became so widely accepted, and how, to borrow his term, the
shadowland of myth and legend eclipsed historical reality so
powerfully. The highwayman who had been more or less com-
pletely forgotten in the years after his death had, over a century
after his demise, taken on a new reality and a totally unexpected
celebrity.

In the early twentieth century it was the Turpin of
Ainsworth's fiction, of the penny dreadfuls, of the stagings of
Dick Turpin's Ride to York, that was firmly lodged in the public's
mind. This situation has not altered, and, indeed, through
film, television, and even pantomime, the Turpin image has
constantly been remodelled and refurbished. With Turpin we
encounter the clear distinction between the type of attempts to
reconstruct historical reality at which historians struggle, and
the historical myth that so often achieves widespread public
currency and triumphs over the historians and their labours.
The term 'myth' is employed loosely here, and both anthropologists and the compilers of dictionaries demand more precise
usage. But historical myth in this context is a set of beliefs
about an aspect of the past that does have a core of reality, but
which is held by most people uncritically as part of their general cultural heritage. Thus Dick Turpin as most of us know
him is clearly a creature of historical myth. Few people know
much of the details of Turpin's life and career. Yet the Turpin
image is readily recognisable, and so too, in so far as it can be

separated from Turpin's, is that of the English highwayman more generally.

If, as anthropologists remind us, myths have a deeper purpose or significance, what can be read into the invocation of Turpin? It is a matter of interest, and, to the academic historian, of concern, that many of the alleged Turpin associations are spurious. The past, with its overtones of heritage and tradition, is obviously a desirable commodity. This 'false' past allows us to buy into something that may never have existed, and to which we may not be really connected, but which, in its inclusiveness, helps us feel safe. This does not, apparently, mean that we have to get the past right.

This takes us beyond the taste for Turpin associations. History, if not quite the new gardening, is a subject that is enjoying something of a vogue. There are numerous history programmes on television, there are a number of history books that have sold exceptionally well recently, a few individual historians have achieved star status, and, more generally, the past, usually described as heritage, is becoming ever more enshrined in a burgeoning number of museums and cognate institutions. It is striking that all of this is progressively marginalising the type of history that is taught, researched, and written about, in academe. Popular history and the heritage industry have become key zones for perpetuating the 'dumbing down' of English culture. History, a demanding and sometimes difficult intellectual pursuit, is being reconstituted as theme park. Much television history – for example, recent series on Elizabeth I or the wives of Henry VIII – has the same cultural resonances as reading *Hello!* magazine: in a reflection of the current obsession with 'celebrity', we are invited briefly into the lives of the great and famous, given a peep-show of their experiences, and then, at the end of the allotted hour, shuffled out again into our more hum-drum existences. The idea that history is a discipline that involves critical discourse, and in which conflicting views inter-play, vanishes. Attempts at confronting the complexity of the past are buried in the production team's agenda, and smothered by a desire to replace reflective opinions by soundbites.

This situation is compounded by the broadsheet newspa-pers. They define themselves against the overt philistinism of the British tabloids, and their readership is at the more intelligent end of the British public. If we retain the notion that historical accuracy is of importance (and there may be some problems with this premise), this lack of concern with such accuracy would be a serious enough matter. Equally serious is the way in which this reading public, which understandably includes very few people with an informed or specialist interest in history, is, via reviews, served up with opinions about history, and directed towards those history books considered worth reading. There are some academic historians reviewing for the broadsheet press, and they, the odd bit of ideological bias, personal animosity, and axe-grinding apart, generally do a good job. But a large propor-tion of reviews of history books are written by people with little specialist knowledge of history or sensitivity to historical tech-niques or the processes of historical research and writing. Some such reviewers do bring a fresh and intelligent perspective to the historical works they are commenting on: for others, the funda-mental desiderata for a good history book is that it should con-tain a minimum of complexity and that, above all, it should be an easy read. Repeatedly in the broadsheet reviews we find the term 'academic' used pejoratively, as if a desire to confront the complexity of the past, attempt difficult explanations, avoid soundbite culture and make qualifications, and display and respect professional competence were utterly damning. For some reason, lack of proper qualifications or technical skill seems to be acceptable, or indeed desirable, among people writing history books or presenting television history in a way in which it would not be acceptable among, for example, dentists or plumbers.

Many of these issues have long been commented on in relation to historical movies. The editor of a book on Hollywood's approach to history, Mark C. Carnes, has some very pertinent observations to make on the subject. 'Even if all imagined pasts are imperfect', he writes, 'their imperfections are distinctive.' Professional historians, he observes with some insight, 'pluck from the muck of the historical records the most solid bits of evidence, mould them into meanings, and usually serve them up as books that, though encrusted with footnotes and redolent of musty archives, can be held and cherished, pondered and disputed'. This process, he contends, is very different from that enshrined in history as told by the movies.

> Hollywood History is different. It fills irritating gaps in the historical record and polishes dulling ambiguities and complexities. The final product gleams, and sears the imagination ... Hollywood History sparkles because it is so morally unambiguous, so devoid of tedious complexity, so *perfect*.

And that perfection, and that moral unambiguity, and that lack of tedium-inducing complexity, frequently depends upon a cheerful (and perhaps sometimes cynical) refusal to let the facts get in the way of a good story.

Twentieth-century Hollywood may be a long way from eighteenth-century highway robbers. Yet many promoters of the popular myth of highwaymen have acknowledged a divergence between their approach to their subject matter, and that which might be taken by the professional or academic historian. Thus Patrick Pringle, author of a book on highwaymen published in 1951, at the end of what is in fact an intelligent, lucid, and well-informed discussion of the myth of the ride to York, comments 'but enough. If we start delving any deeper into the archives we shall find ourselves willy-nilly in the mournful company of the learned historians.' Charles C. Harper, in his *Half-Hours with the Highwaymen*, published in 1908, offers a chilling prospect of the likely fate of works published by this 'mournful company':

> It would be a thankless task to present the highwayman as he really was: a fellow rarely heroic, generally foul-mouthed and cruel, and often cowardly. No novelist would be likely to thank the frank historian for this disservice; and I do not think that the historian who came to the subject in this cold scientific spirit of a demonstrator in surgery would be widely read.

This rather discouraging passage demonstrates a basic tension. Pringle was aware of the need to explore the possibility of getting something right, and Harper was aware that the reality of the highwayman as an historical figure was different from that of popular myth. Yet both of them, for rhetorical reasons or otherwise, felt it necessary to shy away from 'learned historians', in much the same spirit as those reviewers in the broadsheet newspapers who reserve 'academic' as their most damning insult when reviewing works of history.

Thus we arrive at a basic problem, the widespread unwillingness to accept or engage with any level of difficulty or acknowledge any concept of professional expertise in endeavours that are purely intellectual. Is getting history right really so unimportant? And if so, how does this unimportance fit with that ever-increasing public hunger for history, or at least for tasty and easily digestible morsels of the past?

We need to ponder on what it means to 'get history right'. There are, of course, different types of history. Perhaps the most demanding, from the point of view of the historian and the reader alike, is the technical, heavily researched, and very scholarly history that appears in the academic journal, the learned monograph and the edited text. Such publications (and much the same holds true of publications in most other scholarly disciplines) are primarily read by other people working in the discipline, and it is on this level that the discipline really progresses. Yet at least some historians feel that they have a wider remit, and that, as well as (or in some cases instead of) their involvement in this very technical level of research and publication, they should also be writing works that are both technically accomplished enough to be acceptable to the academy and also accessible to the general public. Obviously, this involves pitching what one writes at different levels, but a number of basic rules, such as respect for evidence, attempts at least to get to grips with all relevant documentation, a respect for balance in the approach taken to the subject and a willingness to face complexity and ambiguity in both what is being written about and the materials upon which that writing is based have to be observed. Moreover, most historians would accept that what they write is not, and cannot be, definitive. We try to do the best we can with the materials and time available to us, secure in the knowledge that at some future point somebody else will either juggle the materials we have used in a different way, discover new materials that alter our view of the subject in question, or, since we and our works are all products of the time and culture in which we live, provide a new interpretation.

History, or the past more generally, is something that, in however oblique a way, is of interest to a broad cross-section of the general public. But the fact that this general public does not, and in all honestly perhaps has no need to, bring to its contact with the past the same critical ability as does a professional historian is of some consequence. There is at least the lingering feeling that if the past is worth anything, the past that is on offer should be recreated at as professional and technically skilled a level as possible. Some possible consequences of what might happen if it is not are indicated by those political regimes for which presenting a generally falsified view of the past, and using a falsified and hegemonic view of history in the process, is an essential element in maintaining ideological control. As George Orwell pointed out in *Nineteen Eighty-Four*, controlling the past can be an important element in controlling the present and the future. Promoting a distinctive and ideologically biased view of the past was obviously essential not just in the fictional milieu of Orwell's Oceania, but also in real life states as disparate as Stalin's Russia and the England of Elizabeth I. In Stalin's Russia, images of his early opponents, most notably Trotsky, were literally removed from the historical record by airbrushing photographs. In Elizabeth I's England, Shakespeare, in his history plays, constructed an in many ways fictionalised past whose main function was to justify the legitimacy of the Tudor regime. Even non-totalitarian states are anxious to preserve a certain view of the past, as, for instance, analysis of the history books used in England in the Victorian era demonstrates. Teaching history in schools, indeed, remains a matter of dispute in England and many other countries, demonstrating its conflicting status as a subject that can serve both as a vehicle for a dominant ideology and also as a means of honing critical ability. Studying history, among other things, should encourage a questioning of sources and opinions, and clarity of thought when confronted with questionable data.

Perhaps rather unexpectedly, the story of Dick Turpin and the wider myth of the English highwayman, as well as their intrinsic interest, are replete with problems about how we approach the past, and what part academic history plays in that process. The man whose body lies (if not perhaps exactly where we think it does) in that old cemetery in York has generated both a history and an historical myth that were surely unthought of when he was executed in 1739. Nobody then could have thought that books would be written about Turpin well over two centuries and a half after his death, and that his image would be a widely diffused and widely recognised one, symbolising a now long-gone form of criminality. But fame is a strange commodity, and there is no doubt that Dick Turpin will continue to enjoy it: the historian might be forgiven for thinking that he enjoys it in rather larger measure than he deserves.

NOTES *and* REFERENCES

Chapter 1: York, April 1739

The essential starting point for anybody interested in Turpin is Derek Barlow, *Dick Turpin and the Gregory Gang* (London and Chichester, 1973), which contains exhaustive references to contemporary documentary and newspaper sources. Two problems should, however, be noted with Barlow's use of manuscript sources. Firstly, he modernised and streamlined quotations from them, and, secondly, a number of document reference numbers, and the arrangement of documents within books, etc., have been changed since he wrote. Barlow is, moreover, also somewhat imprecise in his rendition of the titles of printed sources. There is another listing of relevant eighteenth-century newspaper references in what is one of the more thoughtful of the many Turpin biographies, Arty Ash and Julius E. Day, *Immortal Turpin: the authentic History of England's most notorious Highwayman* (London and New York, 1948), pp. 141–2.

The description of Turpin's execution comes from the earliest of his biographies, namely Richard Bayes, *The Genuine History of the life of Richard Turpin, the noted Highwayman, who was executed at York for Horse-Stealing, under the name of John Palmer, on Saturday Ap. 7, 1739* (London, 1739), pp. 32–3. George Cooke's request for reimbursement of expenses is in the Public Record

Office, London (hereafter PRO), T/90/147, f. 317. Arthur Jessop's opinions on the weather are given in *Two Yorkshire Diaries*, ed. C. E. Whiting (Yorkshire Archaeological Society Record Series, 117, 1952), p. 45. Thomas Hadfield being pardoned on condition he turned hangman is reported in *The York Courant*, 10 April 1739.

Patrick J. Nuttgens (ed.), *The History of York: from earliest Times to the Year 2000* (Pickering, 2000) is an overview of the city's history aimed at the general reader; Francis Drake's comments come from his *Eboracum: or the History and Antiquities of the City of York* (London, 1736), pp. 240–41, 287. Biographical details on Drake are given in K. J. Allison's 'Introduction' to the 1978 reproduction of this work.

The letter describing Turpin's conduct in prison, dated 2 March and published in the *General Evening Post* is printed at length in Ash and Day, *Immortal Turpin*, pp. 99–101. Barlow, *Dick Turpin and the Gregory Gang*, p. 383, reports he found it impossible to locate an original copy of this journal. The 'Letter from York' of 23 March was probably much republished in the provincial press of the period: I have quoted it from *The Lancashire Journal with the History of the Holt Bible* of 2 April 1739. The other quotations on Turpin in prison come from Bayes, *Genuine History*, pp. 30, 31–2.

For William Harris's evidence, East Riding Archive Office, Beverley, QSF122/D7; for John Robinson's and Abraham Green's, QSF122/D8; Robert Appleton's account of how Turpin was arrested comes from *The whole Trial of the notorious Highwayman Richard Turpin, at York Assizes, on the 22d Day of March, 1739, before the Hon. Sir William Chapple, Kt, Judge of Assize, and one of his Majesty's Justices of the Court of King's*

Bench. Taken down in Court by Mr. Thomas Kyll, Professor of Short Hand. To which is prefix'd, an exact Account of the said Turpin, from his first coming into Yorkshire, to the time of his being committed to York Castle communicated by Mr Appleton of Beverly, Clerk of the Peace for the East-Riding of the said County. With a Copy of a Letter which Turpin received from his Father, while under Sentence of Death, &c (York, 1739). On the background to his being sent to Beverley, see Barlow, *Dick Turpin and the Gregory Gang*, pp. 346–8. The evidence for this phase of Turpin's life given in later trial proceedings is quoted from the statements of the relevant witnesses as recorded in *The whole Trial of the notorious Highwayman Richard Turpin*.

The list of prisoners awaiting trial used as a wrapper for the Essex Lent assizes of 1739 records that the indictment against John Turpin, charged with horse-theft in Lincolnshire, had been rejected; the indictment survives in the general file for the Home Circuit, Lent 1739, giving the location of the theft as Essex. The indictment was returned *ignoramus*, indicating that the grand jury, whose role it was to screen indictments, did not think that there was a legally sustainable case against John Turpin: PRO, ASSI 94/639, 94/643.

The story of the letter was given in the *General Evening Post* of 8 March 1739, quoted extensively by Ash and Day, *Immortal Turpin*, pp. 99–101, and the evidence given about this incident in later trial proceedings comes from *The whole Trial of the notorious Highwayman Richard Turpin*. Several contemporary publications printed versions of what purported to have been Turpin's letter: their authenticity is discussed and dismissed in Barlow, *Dick Turpin and the Gregory Gang*, pp. 355–9.

For James Smith's statement of 23 February 1739, PRO, SP

36/47/88. For Thomas Place's letter to the Duke of Newcastle, ibid., /89.

For Dudley Ryder's letter to the Duke of Newcastle, PRO, SP 36/47/100.

On the involvement of George Crowle, see Barlow, *Dick Turpin and the Gregory Gang,* pp. 372–6. The letter quoted is in PRO, T/53/40, f. 158. Biographical details on Crowle are given in Romney Sedgwick, *The House of Commons 1715–1754* (2 volumes, London: History of Parliament Trust, 1970), vol. I, pp. 596–7.

The texts of the indictments against Turpin are given by Barlow, *Dick Turpin and the Gregory Gang,* p. 387. The originals form part of PRO, ASSI 44/55. The problems with the accuracy of indictments was highlighted by J. S. Cockburn, 'Early modern Assize Records as historical Evidence', *Journal of the Society of Archivists,* 5 (1975), pp. 215–31.

Details of other offenders tried at the same assize as Turpin are given in the *York Courant* for 10 April. Details of John Stead's age and domicile are given in William Knipe, *Criminal Chronology of York Castle: with a Register of the Criminals capitally convicted and executed at the County Assizes* (York, 1867), p. 47. Sir William Chapple's career is described briefly in *The Dictionary of National Biography*

For Turpin's trial, see *The whole Trial of the notorious Highwayman Richard Turpin*: Creasy's main evidence comes at pp. 4–7, Dawson's at pp. 7–8, Grassby's at p. 9, Saward's at pp. 14–15, Smith's at pp. 11–12, 15–16, 20, and Turpin's comments on the unfairness of his treatment at pp. 17 and 20–21. Unfortunately, the relevant pages of the York Gaol Book for 1736–1762, PRO, ASSI 41/4, are missing, having presumably been removed by an early and unscrupulous hunter of Turpin memorabilia, and hence we are unable to gain an impression of the other business conducted at the assize. Sir George Cooke's accounts confirm that Hadfield and Hollings were reprieved, and give the costs involved in keeping them in custody for forty and forty-six weeks respectively: PRO, T/90/147, f. 317. Recognizances calling on witnesses and accusers to give evidence against those standing trial are preserved in PRO, ASSI 44/55.

The fate of Turpin's corpse after execution is described in Bayes, *Genuine History*, p. 33. For the details on the riot to rescue Turpin's body, see York City Archives, F15 (Sessions Book 11 October 1728–26 October 1744), ff. 193–194v, 197–198; I am grateful to Linda Haywood for bringing this reference to my attention. For the background to popular objections to the dissection of dead criminals, see Peter Linebaugh, 'The Tyburn Riot against the Surgeons', in Douglas Hay *et al.*, *Albion's Fatal Tree: Crime and Society in eighteenth-century England* (London, 1975).

Chapter 2: Highwaymen

Frith recorded the painting of 'Claude Duval' in his *My Autobiography and Reminiscences* (3rd edn, 2 volumes, London 1887), vol. 1, pp 304–6, 317–18. The painting is discussed in Roy Strong, *Recreating the Past: British History and the Victorian Painter* (London, 1978), pp. 43, 60, 93–4: *ibid*, p. 60, notes that Frith would have hated the way in which 'his historical works have been ignored and his achievement assessed almost solely in the light of his contemporary genre compositions'. The description of the incident that inspired the painting can be found in T. B. Macaulay, *The History of England from the Accession of James II* (5 volumes, London, 1849), vol. 1, p. 383.

Many books have been written about highwaymen since the nineteenth-century craze for such works that was caused, as we shall see, by the reinvention of Richard Turpin. Of this, my favourite is Charles G. Harper, *Half-Hours with the Highwaymen: picturesque Biographies and Traditions of the 'Knights of the Road'* (2 volumes, London, 1908). Recent works in this vein include Gillian Spraggs, *Outlaws and Highwaymen: the Cult of the Robber in England from the Middle Ages to the Nineteenth Century* (London, 2001); and David Brandon, *Stand and Deliver: a History of Highway Robbery* (London, 2001).

There has been no full-scale study of late seventeenth- and eighteenth-century highwaymen by an academic historian, although many of the works on crime in this period mention the phenomenon. Jeremy Pocklington, 'Highway Robbery, 1660–1720: Practice, Policies and Perceptions' (M.Phil. thesis, Oxford University, 1997), was consulted, but was found to have little material relevant to the current study. The highwayman image and its foundations in contemporary ephemeral literature are, however, discussed in an excellent work, Lincoln B. Faller, *Turned to Account: the Forms and Functions of Criminal Biography in seventeenth and early eighteenth-century England* (Cambridge, 1987).

Daniel Saddler's robbing of Frances Maskell is recorded in PRO, ASSI 94/639.

The works cited on definitions of highway robbery are: Richard Burn, *The Justice of the Peace, and Parish Officer* (2 volumes, London, 1755 edn), vol. 2, pp. 541, 508–9; Michael Dalton, *The Countrey Justice; containing the Practice of Justices of the Peace out of their Sessions gathered for the better Help of such Justices of Peace, as have not been much conversant in the Study of the Laws of the Realm* (London, 1690 edn), p. 363.

The 1693 Act was 4 and 5 William and Mary, cap. 8, 'An Act for Encouraging the Apprehending of Highwaymen'.

For the seventeenth-century Essex figures, see J. A. Sharpe, *Crime in seventeenth-century England: a County Study* (Cambridge, 1983), pp. 104–6. The arrest of Peter Hall is recorded in *'William Holcroft his Booke': Local Office-Holding in late Stuart Essex*, ed. J. A. Sharpe (Essex Historical Documents, 2, Essex Record Office, Chelmsford, pp. 70–71). For the murder in the course of a highway robbery, see Sharpe, *County Study*, p. 106.

For highway robbery in Surrey, see J. M. Beattie, *Crime and the Courts in England 1660–1800* (Oxford, 1986), pp. 148–61.

The details on various highwaymen are taken from a twentieth-century compendium that reproduces seventeenth- and eighteenth-century accounts, *The Complete Newgate Calendar*, eds. J. L. Rayner and G. T. Crook (5 volumes, London, 1926). The comments on MacLaine's claims to gentility come from *The complete History of James MacLean, the Gentleman Highwayman, who was executed at Tyburn on Wednesday, October 3, 1750, for Robbery in the Highway* (London, 1750), p. 65. The incident in which the pedlar woman had her tongue cut out is cited in Beattie, *Crime and the Courts*, p. 152.

For James Hind's capture, trial and execution (this list is not exhaustive) see: *The Declaration of Captain Hind (Close Prisoner in New-Gate) and his Acknowledgement, Protestation and full Confession at his Examination before the Counsel of State the 10 of this Instant November 1651* (London, 1651); *The humble Petition of James Hind (Close Prisoner in New-Gate). To the Right Honorable the Councell of State: and their Proceedings thereupon* (London, 1651); *The Tryal of Captain James Hind on Friday last, before the Right Honorable the Lord Mayor, and the Judges, at the Sessions in the Old Bayley. With his*

Examination and Confession; and the Manner of his undanted Deport-ment (London, 1651); *The last Will and Testament of James Hind, Highway Robber, now sick to Death in ... Newgate. Full of various Conceits beyond Expectation* (London, 1651); *The Trial of Capt. J. H. ... at the Sessions of the Old Bayley; with his Examination and Confession, etc.* (London, 1651).

Works creating and continuing the Hind tradition include: *A second Discovery of Hind's exploits, or, a further Relation of his Rambles, Robberies and Cheats in England, Ireland, Scotland with his Voyage to Holland* (London, 1651); *A Pill to Purge Melancholy: or, merry Newes from Newgate, wherein is set forth the pleasant Jests, witty Conceits, and excellent Couzenages of Captain James Hind and his Associates, etc.* (London, 1651); *No Jest like a true Jest: being a compendious Record of the merry Life and maddest Exploits of Capt. James Hind, the great Robber of England, etc.* (London, 1674: reprints survive from 1750, 1765, 1775, 1805 and 1817); a ballad, *Captain Hind's Progress and Ramble*, published *c.* 1710; and an undated play, *An excellent Comedy, called the Prince of Prigg's Revels, or the Practices of that grand Thief, Captain James Hind, etc.* The Hind legend was also preserved in the large collections of highwaymen's lives that were published in the eighteenth century, as in the earliest example of this genre, Alexander Smith, *The History of the Lives of the most noted Highway-Men, Foot-Pads, Housebreakers, Shop-Lifts and Cheats of both Sexes, in and about London, and in other Places in Great Britain, for about forty Years Past* (2 volumes, London, 1714), vol. 1, pp. 275-9. The eighteenth-century comments on Hind's reputation come from Charles Johnson, *A General History of the Lives and Adventures of the most famous Highwaymen, Murderers, Street-Robbers &c, to which is added a genuine Account of the Voyages and Plunders of the most notorious Pyrates* (London, 1734), p. 86.

The key work on Duval is *The Mémoires of Monsieur du Vall: containing the History of his Life and Death. Whereunto are annexed his last Speech and Epitaph* (London, 1670: reprinted, 1744). See also *The Life of Deval. Shewing how he came to be a Highway-Man; and how he committed several Robberies afterwards. Together with his Arraignment and Condemnation. As also his Speech and Confession, at the Place of Execution* (London, 1670).

For Duval's dance with the lady, *The Complete Newgate Calendar*, eds. Rayner and Crook, vol. 1, p. 222; on his lying in state, *Mémoires of Monsieur du Vall*, 13; ibid., p. 9, for the quotation on Duval's skill in music, singing, dancing and repartee, and p. 10 for the incident with the baby's bottle; Samuel Butler, *To the Memory of the most renowned Du-Vall: a Pindarick Ode* (London, 1671).

Details on Alexander Smith and his writings are taken from the entry on him in *The Dictionary of National Biography*; J. M. Beattie, *Policing and Punishment in London 1660–1750: Urban Crime and the Limits of Terror* (Oxford, 2001), pp. 372–3, animadverts that it was possibly not coincidental that this work appeared during the post-Treaty of Utrecht crime wave.

On *The Old Bailey Sessions Papers*, see Beattie, *Policing and Punishment in London*, pp. 372–4.

For the quotations on the publishing of highwaymen's lives, see: Smith, *The History of the Lives*, vol. 1, p. i; *Anecdotes, Bon Mots, Traits, Stratagems and Biographical Sketches of the most remarkable Highwaymen, Swindlers, and other daring Adventurers who have flourished, from a very early Period, to the present Time* (London, 1797), p. iii; Charles Johnson, *A General History of the Lives and Adventures*, p. 1.

The context of the *Beggar's Opera* can be examined through

the various essays in Peter Lewis and Nigel Wood (eds.), *John Gay and the Scriblerians* (London and New York, 1988); and Sven M. Armens, *John Gay: Social Critic* (New York, 1966).

For comments on highwaymen and Jacobitism, see Frank McLynn, *Crime and Punishment in Eighteenth-Century England* (Oxford, 1991), pp. 57–8.

For Jack Blewit, *The Complete Newgate Calendar*, eds. Rayner and Crook, vol. 2, pp. 226–30; for Jack Ovet, ibid., vol. 2, pp. 202–5; for Evan Evans, ibid., vol. 2, pp. 208–11; for William Nevison, ibid, vol. 1, pp. 283–92; Nevison's life is commemorated in *The History of the Life & Death of that noted Highwayman Mr William Nevison* (Nottingham, n.d.), a tract probably published in the 1760s but maybe based on an earlier original. For a later celebration of Nevison, see the *Life and Adventures of John William Nevison, the Northern 'Claude Duval'* (Royal Pocket Library, no. 66), a mid nineteenth-century chapbook that ascribes the ride to York to Nevison, and is insistent that Turpin's claims to have performed the feat is a fiction created by the novel *Rookwood*. The other pleasantries noted are taken from McLynn, *Crime and Punishment in Eighteenth-Century England*, p. 61.

For forgers 1750–61, see *The Complete Newgate Calendar*, eds. Rayner and Crook, vol. 3, pp. 190–94, 212–13, 260–61, 285–9.

Daniel Defoe, *A Tour through the whole Island of Great Britain* (Everyman edn: 2 volumes, London, 1962), vol. 1, pp. 104–5; this work was first published in three volumes between 1724 and 1726. For a discussion of this account and earlier traditions of the ride to York, see, e.g., Patrick Pringle, *Stand and Deliver: the Story of the Highwaymen,* Chapter 15, 'Who Rode to York?', where the legend of the ride to York as a noteworthy feat of horsemanship is traced back to 1606 and a rider named John Lepton.

Chapter 3: Crime

The comments on the brutality of the eighteenth-century penal system come from J. H. Plumb, *The First Four Georges* (London, 1956), pp. 20, 16; and V. H. H. Green, *The Hanoverians* (London, 1948), p. 254. Cf. Dorothy Marshall, *Eighteenth-Century England* (London, 1962), p. 243.

Hogarth's print of Tom Idle's execution has been frequently reproduced, e.g., in J. A. Sharpe, *Crime and the Law in English Satirical Prints 1600–1832* (Cambridge, 1986), p. 127. Hogarth's 'Industry and Idleness' series of prints, of which this is part, is discussed in Ronald Paulson, *Popular and Polite Art in the Age of Hogarth and Fielding* (Notre Dame and London, 1979), Chapter 2, 'The Apprentice'; for a full discussion of the print, see the same author's *Hogarth's Graphic Works: First Complete Edition* (2 volumes, New Haven and London, 1965), vol. 1, pp. 200–201.

Bernard de Mandeville, *An Enquiry into the Causes of the Frequent Executions at Tyburn: and a Proposal for some Regulations concerning Felons in Prison, and the good effects to be Expected from them* (London, 1725), pp. 18–37.

The fullest scholarly work on executions in eighteenth-century London is Peter Linebaugh, *The London Hanged: Crime and Civil Society in the Eighteenth Century* (Harmondsworth, 1991). On the crowds visiting Jack Sheppard and MacLaine in prison, for the 1698 observations of the foreign observer, and for other references to Tyburn ceremonies, see Leon Radzinowicz, *A History of English Criminal Law and*

Its Administration from 1750: Volume 1, The Movement for Reform (London, 1948), pp. 190–94.

On the importance of the speech from the scaffold, see J. A. Sharpe, '"Last Dying Speeches": Religion, Ideology and Public Execution in seventeenth-century England', *Past and Present*, 107 (1985), pp. 144–67. On half-hanging, see Radzinowicz, *Movement for Reform*, pp. 190–94.

Although now in many respects overtaken by more recent interpretations, Radzinowicz's *The Movement for Reform* remains an essential guide to the operation of the criminal law in the period of the 'Bloody Code'. J. M. Beattie, *Crime and the Courts in England 1660–1800* (Oxford, 1986), in essence a study of crime and its repression in Surrey, is the best recent study of crime and punishment in the eighteenth century, while the same author's *Policing and Punishment in London 1660–1750: Urban Crime and the Limits of Terror* (Oxford, 2001), is also essential reading. Petty crime in the metropolitan area is analysed by Robert B. Shoemaker, *Prosecution and Punishment: Petty Crime and the Law in London and Rural Middlesex, c. 1660–1725* (Cambridge, 1991). An introduction to the history of crime in this period is provided by J. A. Sharpe, *Crime in Early Modern England, 1550–1750* (2nd edn, London, 1999). The topic has been the subject of a number of works, of varying quality, by popular historians, a recent example being Frank McLynn, *Crime and Punishment in Eighteenth-Century England* (Oxford, 1991).

For long-term changes in levels of execution, see Sharpe, *Crime in Early Modern England*, pp. 90–99, and the same author's *Judicial Punishment in England* (London, 1990), pp. 27–36. For capital sentences in Devon in 1598, see A. H. A. Hamilton, *Quarter Sessions from Queen Elizabeth to Queen Anne* (London,

1878), pp. 30–31; for Jeaffreson's figures, *Middlesex County Records*, ed. J. C. Jeaffreson (Middlesex County Records Society, 4 volumes, 1886–92), vol. 2, pp. xvii–xxi.

The 1718 Transportation Act and its workings form the subject matter of Roger A. Ekirch, *Bound for America: the Transportation of British Convicts to the Colonies, 1718–1775* (Oxford, 1987).

The importance of selectivity in the punishment of criminals, and its role in the wider workings of the punishment system in eighteenth-century England, is discussed in Douglas Hay, 'Property, Authority and the Criminal Law', in Douglas Hay *et al.*, *Albion's Fatal Tree: Crime and Society in Eighteenth-Century England* (London, 1975). The felon expressing surprise at his fate is quoted in Sharpe, *Crime in Early Modern England*, p. 249.

There has recently been a number of works on the history of London, of varying quality: Peter Earle, *A City Full of People: Men and Women of London, 1650–1750* (London, 1994), describes life in the city in the period relevant to our study. Some idea of the physical nature of the London of the 1730s is provided by Elizabeth McKellar, *The Birth of Modern London: the Development and Design of the City 1660–1720* (Manchester, 1999).

The quotation from Henry Fielding is from his *Enquiry into the Increase into the Causes of the late Increase of Robbers, &c.*, with some *Proposals for Remedying this growing Evil* (London, 1751), p. 116.

For Henry Norris, see *Justice in Eighteenth-Century Hackney: the Justicing Notebook of Henry Norris and the Hackney Petty Sessions Book*, ed. Ruth Paley (London Record Society, vol. 28, 1991); the cases cited are at pp. 15–16, 2, 35–6, 36 respectively; the breakdown of Norris's business comes from Shoemaker, *Prosecution and Punishment*, Table 3.1, pp. 44–5.

Comments on those hanged at Tyburn in the period 1703–72 are based on Linebaugh, *The London Hanged*, Chapter 3, 'Tyburnology: the Sociology of the Condemned'.

The description of Wild's career rests heavily on Gerald Howson, *Thief-Taker General: Jonathan Wild and the Emergence of Crime and Corruption as a Way of Life in Eighteenth-Century England* (London, 1970). The quotation from the *London Journal* is given ibid., p. 251.

On the development of rewards as a vital part of law enforcement, see Beattie, *Policing and Punishment in London 1660–1750,* pp. 376–84; for the details of payments in Middlesex in the early 1730s, ibid., pp. 402–3.

On criminal gangs, see Beattie, *Crime and the Courts in England*, pp. 156–69.

Chapter 4: The Essex Gang and Its Aftermath
The 1731 affadavit by the Verderers of Waltham Forest is PRO, SP 36/22/136; Newcastle's proclamation, PRO, SP 36/23/12. My description of offences in Waltham Forest in the early 1730s, and the composition of the deer-stealers, is based on the fuller account given by Derek Barlow, *Dick Turpin and the Gregory Gang* (London, 1973), pp. 1–39. For an important study of deer-stealing in another area and its broader implications, see E. P. Thompson, *Whigs and Hunters: the Origin of the Black Act* (London, 1975).

Parish Registers for Hempstead are held in the Essex Record Office, Chelmsford, D/P 314.

The Political State of Great Britain (hereafter cited as *The Political State*), vol. 49, pp. 24–7 for the Essex gang's early robberies.

For the robbery at Chingford, Barlow, *Dick Turpin and the Gregory Gang*, pp. 48–50; for the Barking Robbery, *The Political State*, vol. 49, pp. 24–7; also depositions, PRO, SP 36/33/1 (this document is also marked 146 and 149 in pencil), ff. 3, 4. For the attack on the William Mason residence, *The Political State*, vol. 49, p. 27; also depositions, PRO, SP 36/33, ff. 128–34

For the Charlton robbery, *The Political State*, vol. 49, p. 111; for the Croydon robbery, Barlow, *Dick Turpin and the Gregory Gang*, p. 70; for the Great Parndon and Loughton robberies, *Reid's Weekly Journal*, 1 February 1735 and 8 February 1735 respectively.

Bladen's letter to Tylney, PRO, SP 36/33/136 (Barlow gives this as /163–4; the relevant document is stamped 163–4, probably an indication that the file has been reorganised since Barlow wrote).

The whereabouts in London of the Essex gang early in 1735 are given by Barlow, *Dick Turpin and the Gregory Gang*, p. 82; the Earlsbury Farm robbery is described and referenced, ibid., pp. 83–99, and that at William Francis's farm, ibid., pp. 94–9. The Earlsbury Farm robbery is described in *The Political State*, vol. 49, pp. 240–41, which also mentions a number of similar robberies in the London area.

A copy of Newcastle's proclamation of 8 February 1735 survives in PRO, SP 44/128/345.

The account the arrest of Fielder, Rose and Wheeler comes from *The Political State*, vol. 49, p. 242. The alternative account is given and discussed in Barlow, *Dick Turpin and the Gregory Gang*, p. 100, citing *The Daily Post* of 12 February 1735.

The arrest of Rose, Brazier and Walker is described and the numerous relevant sources discussed in Barlow, *Dick Turpin and the Gregory Gang*, pp. 132–6. The descriptions of the gang come from the *London Gazette* of 18–22 February 1735. The trials of Rose, Fielder, Saunders and Walker are described by Barlow, *Dick Turpin and the Gregory Gang*, pp. 151–9. The indictments against Jasper Gregory survive in PRO, ASSI 94/580.

For the Essex and Brockley robberies, Barlow, *Dick Turpin and the Gregory Gang*, pp. 128–32. For the activities and arrest of Samuel and Jeremy Gregory, *The Old Whig*, 15 May 1735 (cited extensively by Barlow, *Dick Turpin and the Gregory Gang*, pp. 176–8); *The Political State*, vol. 49, pp. 462–3; and PRO, T.53/58, ff. 196v–7; T.53/59, f. 44, two bodies of documentation that give details of the rewards given to those who had helped apprehend the Gregory brothers.

Samuel Gregory's trial and execution is described in Barlow, *Dick Turpin and the Gregory Gang*, pp. 207–9; for a description of his conduct before and at his execution, see *The Political State*, vol. 50, p. 8. The circumstances of Herbert Haines's arrest are reconstructed from details of the rewards awarded to Henry Palmer, James Freeland and John Wheeler, PRO, T53/39, ff. 271–2. For the indictments against him, PRO, ASSI 94/583. A newspaper account of his conduct before his death is quoted by Barlow, *Dick Turpin and the Gregory Gang*, p. 219.

PRO, T/53/38, ff. 406–7, a petition from Dyson Green, Francis Francis and Nicholas Greaves [sic] for a reward for their part in the arrest of John Jones gives a detailed account of the circumstances of his apprehension; see also *Justice in Eighteenth-Century Hackney: the Justicing Notebook of Henry Norris and the Hackney Petty Sessions Book*, ed. Ruth Paley (London Record Society, vol. 28, 1991), p. 32. The indictment against Jones survives in PRO, ASSI 94/593.

For the April 1735 robberies, Barlow, *Dick Turpin and the Gregory Gang*, p. 213; see also Ash and Day, *Immortal Turpin*, pp. 37–9. For the July 1735 proclamation against highwaymen, PRO, SP 44/128/392–3`. The account of the robbery of Mr Vane is given in the *London Evening Post*, 10–12 July 1735, as is that of Mr Omar. Rowden's downfall is described, and fully referenced, in Barlow, *Dick Turpin and the Gregory Gang*, pp. 240–44, 301–5, 317–20, 328–9.

On Wheeler's death, ibid., p. 327. Thomas Cavanagh's claim for expenses is preserved in PRO, SP 44/83/290.

The sources relating to Turpin's supposed visit to the Netherlands are discussed in Barlow, *Dick Turpin and the Gregory Gang*, pp. 244–9.

On Turpin's wife in Hertford gaol, *The Political State*, vol. 53, p. 235; PRO, ASSI 94/608.

On the theft of Whitestockings and the death of Matthew King, see Richard Bayes, *The Genuine History of the Life of Richard Turpin, the noted Highwayman, who was executed at York for Horse-theft, under the Name of John Palmer, on Saturday Ap. 7 1739* (London, 1739), pp. 17–18. Other sources relating to this incident are discussed in Barlow, *Dick Turpin and the Gregory Gang*, pp. 268–80. The varying accounts of Thomas Morris's death are similarly discussed, ibid., pp. 280–93.

The opinions of the inhabitants of Epping Forest are given in *Reid's Weekly Journal*, 14 May 1737, cited by Barlow, *Dick Turpin and the Gregory Gang*, p. 288.

The proclamation offering a £200 reward for Turpin and giving a description of him appeared in *The London Gazette* for 25–28 June 1737.

Chapter 5: The Man from Manchester

Evidence of Manchester's growth is given in Martin Hewitt, *The Emergence of Stability in the Industrial City: Manchester, 1832–67* (Aldershot, 1996), Chapter 1, 'Manchester: Economic Growth and Social Structure'. The quotation from the observer of 1848 is given ibid., p. 23. John Aiken's comments on Manchester come from his *A Description of the Country from thirty to forty Miles round Manchester* (London, 1795), p. 192.

The standard work on Ainsworth, which contains extensive quotations from primary materials dealing with his life, is S. M. Ellis, *William Harrison Ainsworth and his Friends* (2 volumes, London, 1911). W. E. Axon, *William Harrison Ainsworth: a Memoir* (London, 1902) is a brief account of Ainsworth's life, developed from Axon's earlier entry on Ainsworth in *The Dictionary of National Biography*. For a more recent study, which is especially helpful in placing Ainsworth's writings in the literary context of their period, see George J. Worth, *William Harrison Ainsworth* (New York, 1972). See also Harold Locke, *A Bibliographical Catalogue of the Published Novels and Ballads of William Harrison Ainsworth* (London, 1925).

The account of the Ainsworth family and of Ainsworth's early life is based heavily on Ellis, *William Harrison Ainsworth and Friends*, and Axon, *A Memoir*. On his involvement with John Ebers and his marrying Fanny Ebers, see Ellis, *William Harrison Ainsworth and Friends*, vol. 1, pp. 130, 149–50, 156–7. The comment on Ainsworth's apparent lack of prospects in 1831 is given ibid., vol. 1, p. 229.

On the Gothic novel, see Maggie Kilgour, *The Rise of the Gothic Novel* (London, 1995), and such pioneering works as Devendra Prasad Varma, *The Gothic Flame: Being a History of* the Gothic Novel in England (London, 1957). On Ann Radcliffe, see the entry on her in Lorna Sage (ed.), *The Cambridge Guide to Women's Writing in English* (Cambridge, 1999), p. 518. A good introduction to the historical novel is Avrom Fleishman, *The English Historical Novel: Walter Scott to Virginia Woolf* (Baltimore and London, 1972), while Sir Walter Scott receives full treatment in John MacQueen, *The Rise of the Historical Novel* (*The Enlightenment and Scottish Literature*, vol. 2, Edinburgh, 1989). Another genre feeding into *Rookwood* was the book-length crime fiction of the period, well described in Keith Hollingsworth, *The Newgate Novel* (Detroit, 1963).

Ainsworth's account of how *Rookwood* was written is given in a 'Preface', dated Kensal Manor House, 15 December 1849, which was usually included in editions of the novel published after that date. The edition of *Rookwood* consulted was the one-volume fifth edition, in Bentley's Standard Novel Series, of 1837. The main passages quoted come from p. 30 (on Rookwood Place); pp. 56–7 ('who he was ...'); pp. 196–7 ('rash daring ... '); pp. 62–3 ('I don't see how it can be otherwise ...'); p. 64 ('England, Sir, has reason ...'); p. 293 ('a noted high tobygloak ...'); p. 318 ('By God, I will do it ...'); p. 331 ('His blood spins ...'); pp. 326–7 (description of Black Bess); p. 329 ('and thou, too, brave Bess ...'); pp. 354–5 (death of Black Bess).

The 1808 pamphlet connecting Turpin with the ride to York is discussed in Derek Barlow, *Dick Turpin and the Gregory Gang* (London, 1973), pp. 444–9; Horace Smith's ballad is noted in Charles G. Harper, *Half-Hours with the Highwaymen: picturesque Biographies and Traditions of the 'Knights of the Road'* (2 volumes, London, 1908), vol. 1, pp. 229–31.

The last case of 'mounted highway robbery' was dated at 1831 in *First Report of the Commissioners appointed to Inquire as to the best Means of Establishing an efficient Constabulary Force in the Counties of England and Wales* (London: HMSO, 1839), p. 46.

On reviews of *Rookwood*, see Ellis, *William Harrison Ainsworth and Friends*, vol. 1, pp. 256–8; on its early publishing history, ibid., vol. 2, pp. 358–60, and Locke, *Bibliographical Catalogue*, pp. 5–7.

For Ellis's comments on the Ainsworths' marital problems and his setting up house with Touchet and Buckley, *William Harrison Ainsworth and Friends*, vol. 1, p. 270; for the quotations about his looks, ibid., vol. 1, pp. 260–61, 262.

On the impact of Ainsworth's *Jack Sheppard*, see Worth, *William Harrison Ainsworth*, p. 37. One student of the relevant literature of the period describes this work as 'the high point of the Newgate novel as entertainment': Hollingsworth, *Newgate Novel*, p. 132. It is noteworthy that after the hostile reactions to *Jack Sheppard*, which had been preceded by some similarly hostile comments on the portrayal of Turpin in *Rookwood*, Ainsworth never again returned to criminal themes in his novels (indeed, a projected novel on Claude Duval was dropped) and limited himself to historical stories. Interestingly, a review of the first serial episode of Ainsworth's *Tower of London* in *The Times* of 31 December 1839 expressed the hope that the author would not ruin the work 'by converting the publication into that "thieves literature" he has had the bad taste to delight in cultivating'.

Frederic Chapman's account of Browning's meeting Answorth is recorded in Ellis, *William Harrison Ainsworth and Friends*, vol. 2, p. 264, while Ainsworth's steady decline is described in detail in that work. His final visit to Manchester is described at length, ibid., vol. 2, pp. 320–38, and his death, ibid., pp. 341–3. His funeral is noted in *The Times* of 6 January 1882 and 10 January 1882.

Chapter 6: Turpin Hero

NB: I have not given references here to ephemeral literature for which adequate details are given in the text.

The 'very bad lad's' conversation with the prison governor is reported in James Greenwood, *The Seven Curses of London* (London, 1869), pp. 114–15.

Henry Downes Miles's dramatic description of the death of Black Bess comes in his *Dick Turpin* (4th edn, London, 1844), p. 347.

On dramatisations of *Rookwood*, and the continuing popularity of *Dick Turpin's Ride*, see S. M. Ellis, *William Harrison Ainsworth and his Friends* (2 volumes, London, 1911), vol. 1, p. 258. For Hardy's description, see *Far from the Madding Crowd*, ed. John Bayley (London, 1975), pp. 347–53.

On the background to the Victorian children's toy theatre, and the role of the Skelt family in its history, see George Speight, *Juvenile Drama: the History of the Engish Toy Theatre* (London, 1946).

My account of 'penny bloods' and 'penny dreadfuls' leans heavily on Louis James, *Fiction for the Working Man, 1830–1850* (Oxford, 1963), and idem, *Print and the People* (London, 1976). Adjacent themes are addressed in Peter Haining, *A Pictorial History of Horror Stories* (London, 1985), while one of the key myths is analysed in the same author's *The Mystery and Horrible Murders of Sweeney Todd, the Demon Barber of Fleet Street* (London, 1979). The items brought together by Barry Ono are cata‑ logued and briefly described in Elizabeth James and Helen R. Smith, *Penny Dreadfuls and Boys' Adventures: the Barry Ono Col‑ lection of Victorian Popular Literature in the British Library* (Lon‑ don, 1998), another work upon which I have drawn for my account here. Connections between this literature and delin‑ quency is discussed in Patrick A. Dunae, 'Penny Dreadfuls: late nineteenth‑century Boy's Literature and Crime', *Victorian Studies*, 22, (1978–9), pp. 133–50.

For James Greenwood on *Hounslow Heath,* see his *The Wilds of London* (London, 1874), p. 164; for Arthur L. Hayward, see his *The Boys Book of Highwaymen* (London, 1931), pp. v–vi.

For York Castle Museum's website, which at the time of writing features a Dick Turpin quiz, see *http://www.york.gov.uk/ heritage/museums/castle*; for the York Dungeon, *http://www. yorkshirenet.co.uk/yorkdungeon/ydnew97.htm*; for Bishopthorpe Palace, *http://www.bishopthorpepalace.co.uk/greathall.html*; for drinking in Selby pubs, *http://www.selbynet.co.uk/abbey/town.html*.

Turpin associations listed in local heritage and pub websites are too numerous to be detailed individually, and further infor‑ mation on them should be gained by searching under the names given.

The website listing Turpin's connection with sausage‑ making seems to have become defunct since the research for this chapter was initiated, but for the society's homepage, see *web.ukonline/sausappr.htm*. For the Dick Turpin pubs and bars outside England mentioned, see *http://hilton.org.uk/peter/bordeaux _guide/night‑life.shtml*; *http://www.dickturpin.com/docs/main.htm*; *http:// travel.roughguides.com/planning…Dining.asp/JournalID=4889& EntryID=3950.*

The pre-website traditions are cited in: Charles G. Harper, *Half-Hours with the Highwaymen: picturesque Biographies and Traditions of the 'Knights of the Road'* (2 volumes, London, 1908), vol. 1, pp. 237–8; Doris Jones-Baker, *The Folklore of Hertfordshire* (London, 1977), pp. 40–41; Arty Ash and Julius E. Day, *Immortal Turpin: the authentic History of England's most notorious Highwayman* (London and New York, 1948), p. 78; and W. M. Baines, *Old Naburn* (n.p.: Yorkshire Gazette Office, 1895), p. 103.

For Turpinalia at the Three Tuns in Cambridge and the Coach and Horses in Clerkenwell, Ash and Day, *Immortal Turpin*, p. 8.

On Arthur Geoffrey Campion, see *http://www.bookpalace.com/acatalog/Home_Geoff_Campion_Art_167.html*.

The text of Noyes's 'The Highwayman' is widely available: I consulted Alfred Noyes, *Collected Poems in One Volume* (London, 2nd edn, 1963), pp. 11–14. On the writing of the poem, see Alfred Noyes, *Two Worlds for Memory* (London and New York, 1953), pp. 30–31; the possible association with *Rookwood* is noted ibid., p. 3.

The Turpin games are noted in two old toy dealers' websites: *http://www.kiddstoys.co.uk/dturpin.htm*; and *http://www.toycollectors.fsnet.co.uk/bin/dickturp.htm*. The Turpin cigarette card is noted in a description of a set of twenty-five cards on 'Pirates and Highwaymen' issued in 1926 by Lambert and Butler given by *http://www.franklyncards.com/one/pirate.htm*.

Porcelain figures showing Turpin are listed in various dealers' websites, e.g: *http://shirleesvictorianhouse.com/daltmug1.htm*; *http://www.ewolfs.com/past_auctions/oct_art/418-427.html*; *http://doult.com/Dick-Turpin.htm*; *http://www.davidweatherford.com/1363-*

076.html; and *http://www.wooleyandwallis.co.uk/Catalogues/ pg28110/page11.htm*. The 'Dick Turpin' adult novelty item can be viewed on *http://www.gifts4anyone.co.uk/acatalog/dick_turpin. htm*.

For a typical version of 'Turpin Hero', in this case entitled 'Turpin and the Lawyer', see Alfred Williams, *Folk Songs of the Upper Thames* (London, 1923), p. 100. The same work, ibid., p. 101, gives a song entitled 'Dick Turpin's Ride'. On the post-*Rookwood* broadside ballads, see the works listed under 'Turpin, Richard, 1706–1739', in the Bodleian Library *allegro* Catalogue of Ballads, *http://bodley24.bodley.ox.ac.uk/cgi-bi…4.48624:49276: 55762&index=3&db=ballads*. Derek Barlow, *Dick Turpin and the Gregory Gang* (London, 1973), p. 313, gives part of a version of 'Turpin Hero', as do Ash and Day, *Immortal Turpin*, pp. 128–9. James Joyce's acquaintance with 'Turpin Hero', and his comments on the narrative structure of the song, are noted in the 'Introduction' to James Joyce, *Stephen Hero*, ed. Theodore Spencer (revised edn, London, 1956), p. 19. The earliest known song dealing with Dick Turpin is given at the end of a pamphlet of 1737, *New News; great and wonderful News from London in an uproar; or a How and Cry after the great Turpin, with his Escape into Ireland* (London, 1737), pp. 7–8. This song is noteworthy in offering what is probably the earliest assertion that Turpin robbed from the rich to give to the poor.

For Tom Mix's career and filmography, see *The International Dictionary of Film and Filmakers 3, Actors and Actresses*, ed. Amy L. Unterburger (3rd edn, Detroit, 1997), pp. 829–32. The video of Mix's *Dick Turpin* can still be bought in the United States. The performance of *Dick Turpin* at the Fox Fullerton Theater is noted in the relevant section of a Fullerton Heritage website (*http://www.fullertonheritage.org/Advocacy_Issues/foxhistory. htm*), which gives full bibliographical references. Other websites mentioning Turpin films include *http:britishpictures.com/stars/ Marriot.htm*; *http://www.britishpictures.com/stars/Elvey.htm*; *http:// www.wayoutwest.org/finlayson/films.html*; *wysiwyg://49/http://www. hollywood.com/movies/fullcast/movie/248158*; Ash and Day, *Immortal Turpin*, p. 140, mention an early British film on Turpin starring Matheson Lang. Films dealing with highwayman or Turpin themes are noted in Leslie Halliwell, *Halliwell's Film Guide* (7th edn, 1990), pp. 275, 468, 570. *Carry On Dick* has been released on video, CC1075/VEA03239; the comments on it come from Nigel Gearing's review in *Monthly Film Bulletin*, vol. 41, no. 487 (August 1974), pp. 170–71.

Richard O'Sullivan's *Dick Turpin* television series is commemorated in a tribute page, *http://website.lineone.net/~mduq/ series.htm*, while details of O'Sullivan's career are given in a related site, *http://website.lineone.net/mduq/richard2.htm*.

On music hall sketches featuring the Turpin story, see Ash and Day, *Immortal Turpin*, pp. 139–40. Quotations concerning York's Riding Lights Theatre Company's *Dick Turpin* come from a contemporary publicity leaflet in my possession.

Conclusion

On legends on the Great North Road, S. M. Ellis, *William Harrison Ainsworth and his Friends* (2 volumes, London, 1911), vol. 1, pp. 237–8.

Mark C. Carnes (ed.), *Past Imperfect: History according to the Movies* (London, 1996), pp. 9, 100, 102.

Patrick Pringle, *Stand and Deliver: the Story of the Highwaymen* (London, 1951), p. 144. Charles C. Harper, *Half-Hours* with the Highwaymen: picturesque Biographies and Traditions of the 'Knights of the Road' (2 volumes, London, 1908), vol. 1, p. vii.

For the content of Victorian school history textbooks, see Valerie E. Chancellor, *History for their Masters: Opinion in the English History Textbook 1800–1914* (Bath, 1970).

INDEX

A

Adams, William, 71
Aiken, John, 140–41
Ainsworth family, 141–2;
    Ann (née Harrison), 141;
    Anne Blanche, 145, 169;
    Emily, 145; Clara, 169;
    Fanny (née Ebers), 145,
    163, 164; Sarah (née Wells),
    169; Thomas, 141–3
Ainsworth, William Harrison,
    birth, 141; childhood and
    youth, 142–4; death, 169;
    post *Rookwood* career,
    161–70; posthumous
    reputation, 169–70; writing
    style in *Rookwood*, 153–4;
    mentioned, 174, 191, 193,
    209, 210; *see also Rookwood*
Allen, Thomas, 51
America, American Colonies,
    86, 90, 103, 126, 127, 128
American Independence, War
    of, 90
Appleton, Robert, 11, 12–13,
    15
Apsley Guise, 186
Arkwright, Richard, 140
Arnott, Robert, 46–7
Aston, James Partingdon, 144

Aston Munslow, 193
Ayliffe, John, 71

B

Bagshot Heath, 44, 45, 196
Baker, Jane, 36; William, 71
Barkwith, Thomas, 45
Barlow, Derek, 158
Barnes Common, 129, 130
Bartram, Richard, 122
Basingstoke, 186
Baxter, John, 16
Bayes, Richard, 133–5
Bedlam, 77
Berkshire, 50
Bethell, Hugh, 12
Bird, Jack, 46
Black Bess, 7, 9, 35, 138,
    156–7, 158–9, 174–5, 176,
    177, 186, 192, 196, 208
Blackburne, Lancelot, 185
Blackerby, Nathaniel, 122
Blackheath, 59
Bladen, Martin, 114
Blandford, 47
Blessington, Lady Marguerite,
    162
Blewitt, Jack, 48, 66–7
'Bloody Code', 89
Bonnet, Ned, 46